STARTING WITH KIERKEGAARD

Continuum's *Starting with . . .* series offers clear, concise and accessible introductions to the key thinkers in philosophy. The books explore and illuminate the roots of each philosopher's work and ideas, leading readers to a thorough understanding of the key influences and philosophical foundations from which his or her thought developed. Ideal for first-year students starting out in philosophy, the series will serve as the ideal companion to study of this fascinating subject.

Available now:

Starting with Berkeley, Nick Jones

Starting with Derrida, Sean Gaston

Starting with Descartes, C. G. Prado

Starting with Hegel, Craig B. Matarrese

Starting with Heidegger, Tom Greaves

Starting with Hobbes, George MacDonald Ross

Starting with Leibniz, Roger Woolhouse

Starting with Locke, Greg Forster

Starting with Mill, John R. Fitzpatrick

Starting with Nietzsche, Ullrich Haase

Starting with Rousseau, James Delaney

Starting with Sartre, Gail Linsenbard

Starting with Wittgenstein, Chon Tejador

Forthcoming:

Starting with Hume, Charlotte R. Brown and William Edward Morris

Starting with Kant, Andrew Ward

Starting with Merleau-Ponty, Katherine Morris

STARTING WITH KIERKEGAARD

PATRICK SHEIL

Continuum International Publishing Group

The Tower Building
11 York Road
London SE1 7NX

80 Maiden Lane
Suite 704
New York, NY 10038

www.continuumbooks.com

British Library Cataloguing-in-Publication Data
A catalogue record for this book is available from the British Library.

ISBN: HB: 978–1–8470–6580–3
PB: 978–1–8470–6581–0

Library of Congress Cataloguing-in-Publication Data
Sheil, Patrick.
Starting with Kierkegaard/Patrick Sheil.
p. cm.
Includes bibliographical references and index.
ISBN 978-1-84706-581-0 (pbk.) – ISBN 978-1-84706-580-3 (hardback)
1. Kierkegaard, Søren, 1813–1855. I. Title.
B4377.S427 2011
198′.9–dc22
2010027902

Typeset by RefineCatch Limited, Bungay, Suffolk
Printed and bound in Great Britain

CONTENTS

PREFACE

Thank you for picking up *Starting with Kierkegaard*. This book aims to provide an accessible and balanced account of a unique but vastly influential philosopher, and also to make the activity of studying Kierkegaard's writings welcoming for people who may not have a background in either philosophy or theology. Kierkegaard put his own name to some of his works while publishing others under pseudonyms. In *Starting with Kierkegaard*, we will be looking at the signed works just as much as at the pseudonymous ones. The latter have sometimes been concentrated upon at the expense of the former; this book attempts to counteract the tendency.

Parts of this book were based on and/or developed out of a paper on Kierkegaard and St Paul presented at the AGM of the UK Søren Kierkegaard Society on Saturday 3 May 2008, at Christ Church Oxford, hosted by George Pattison. However, it was my intention to write something for that occasion that could also feature in this book. All other parts of the writing were developed for this book alone and have not appeared in any other form.

Some readers may only have immediate use for certain chapters of *Starting with Kierkegaard*. I therefore give titles of works in Danish after the first mention of any work by Kierkegaard in each chapter. The idea is that readers will be able to read chapters in isolation or in the order that best suits their needs. That said, the book does follow a structure, and the structure is as follows: a historical and biographical context chapter, an introduction to some of the pivotal Kierkegaardian concepts, three chapters on three topic-areas that can be seen to correspond to each of the famous Kierkegaardian 'spheres', and finally a chapter on community and society. Full details of the texts referred to can be found in the bibliography.

A number of people have given me invaluable support. David Avital, Sarah Campbell, Nicholas Church, Tom Crick, John O'Donovan and other members of the team at Continuum Books have been caring, attentive and patient. The Continuum team was especially supportive when the manuscript was in its final stages, as were the people at RefineCatch: Donna White, Kirsty Holmes and Kevin Eaton.

Lisa Turner encouraged me to return to the study of the New Testament, and this has helped me to write the book I wanted to write: one that would bring out the philosophical importance of Kierkegaard's religious writings for those embarking on a reading of his works. I am also grateful to Lisa for the many theological discussions that we had over the period of time during which I was preparing the first draft of this book. As a result of those conversations with Lisa, and with Will Punchard (especially through the summer of 2008), I developed the habit of reading Kierkegaard's religious discourses and 'deliberations' alongside the biblical verses to which they relate. Hugh Pyper has also inspired and influenced me on that front.

The published work of the people I got to know through the fortnightly Kierkegaard seminar set up in Cambridge by George Pattison at King's College has continued to inspire me – Steven Shakespeare's *Kierkegaard, Language and the Reality of God* and Clare Carlisle's *Kierkegaard: A Guide for the Perplexed* are just a couple of examples – as has the work of John Lippitt. Lippitt's many insights into Kierkegaard, no less weighty for being nimbly and crisply delivered, make his books fine models of academic writing. Anthony Rudd's *Kierkegaard and the Limits of the Ethical* has also helped me, as has *Love's Grateful Striving* by M. Jamie Ferreira.

Margaret and Richard Widdess and their sons Patrick and Will have supported my efforts and discussed the direction and progress of the book with me on many occasions. Philip Mularo has encouraged me throughout and has often discussed the major themes with me as well as providing technical support on a regular basis. I have had great moral support from Philippa King and from various members of the congregation at St Giles in Cambridge. Jeanette Blair sent me a number of key texts that enabled me to make progress with this project.

Other friends and associates whose kindness and good counsel have inspired me along the way include Tom Adams, Katie Amy, Tom

Angier, Michele Austin, James Bell, Helen Berrey, Kym Birch, Karl Bishop, Lillian Bixler, Pete de Bolla, Victor Bond, Toby Bowcock, Ben Brogan, Andrew Brown, Janet Bunker, Jonathan Burt, Una Carson, Darren Collins, Geoff Coppock, Simon Coppock, Andy Corrigan, Edward Crawshaw, Zoë Crawshaw, Andrew Davey, John and Keith Dixon, John and Pat Drew, Roger Drew, Gabriela Drobčinská, Elly Eyers, Ruth Eveleigh, Helen Fowler, Julia Frank, Neil Goryn, Steve Gothard, Signe Gundersen, Marcus Gynn, Trish Harewood, Stewart Harris, Sarah Henley, Jon Hesk, Shannon Hogan, Ian Hogg, Jon House, Jenny Huguet, Edgar Jasper, Graham Kendall, Martin Lawson, Hannah Lee, Ben Lund, Cynthia Lund, Tom Lyons, Jon Mair, Nikki Maoz, Sue Martin, Andy and Laura Mathers, John Moreira, Andy Nash, Paddy O'Donovan, Simon Owens, Barney Palfrey, Natalie Palmer, Sandra Papworth, Sylvia Pick, Simon Podmore, Jocelyn Pye, Hugh Pyper, Katherine Rager, Peregrine Rand, Ank Rigelsford, Helen and Sammy Rosenberg, Naomi Rosenberg, Ed Scott, Tim Shakesby, Adrian Smith, William Smith, Gez Wyn Story, Erika and Martin Swales, Susan Swannell, Michael Talibard, Ashley Tellis, Laura Timms, Chris and Olivia Thatcher, Kenneth Thirsk, Walter Thompson, Fiona and Suzy Tooke, Richard Trueman, Jamie Turnbull, Jay Vibert, Mike Weston, Lorna Whittle, James Wiley, Rachel Winton, Alasdair Wright, Mark and Maxine Wyatt, Ace Wyld and Ant Wyn.

Above all, my Mum and Dad, Joan and Dan Sheil, have been immensely supportive and encouraging throughout the preparation of yet another manuscript on Kierkegaard, as have my very dear partner Barbara Baron, and her parents, Derek and Joan Baron.

Last but not least, I should say that I am privileged to have been present at many of the 'Philosopher King's' meetings, chaired by Hallvard Lillehammer, in the days when Peter Lipton was a regular participant, including the last session that he attended. A very gracious man of tremendous warmth, originality and humour, Peter was always determined to make philosophy open and available to everybody. No contribution to a philosophical discussion, however flawed and faltering, was irrelevant to him. Peter Lipton was and is an inspiration to us all and it is to his memory that this book is dedicated.

ABBREVIATIONS

The following abbreviations accompanied by page numbers are used in the text referring to English translations of writings by Søren Kierkegaard. In the main I have used the Princeton editions of Kierkegaard's works, the majority of which are translations with introductions by Howard V. Hong and Edna H. Hong. Page references preceded by the abbreviation 'Han.' will appear before the standard references to the Princeton editions wherever Alastair Hannay's translation of the work in question has been quoted. The only exception is 'PJS' which will automatically indicate a Hannay translation. What follows is not a complete list of Kierkegaard's works (such a list can be found in the bibliography), but of works referred to in this book.

BA	*The Book on Adler*
CA	*The Concept of Anxiety*
CDCLA	*Christian Discourses: The Crisis and a Crisis in the Life of an Actress*
CI	*The Concept of Irony*
COR	*The Corsair Affair*
CUP	*Concluding Unscientific Postscript to* Philosophical Fragments
EOI	*Either/Or (Part I)*
EOII	*Either/Or (Part II)*
EO	*Either/Or (Parts I and II, lightly abridged)* (Alastair Hannay translation)
EPW	*Early Polemical Writings*
EUD	*Eighteen Upbuilding Discourses*
FT/R	*Fear and Trembling* and *Repetition*
GS	*The Gospel of Sufferings*

JP	*Søren Kierkegaard's Journals and Papers*
LD	*Letters and Documents*
LY	*Søren Kierkegaard's Journals: The Last Years 1853–1855* (Ronald Gregor Smith translation)
M	*'The Moment' and Late Writings*
PA	*The Present Age* (as introduced by Walter Kaufmann)
PJS	*Papers and Journals: A Selection* (Alastair Hannay translation)
P/WS	*Prefaces/Writing Sampler*
PC	*Practice in Christianity*
PF/JC	*Philosophical Fragments* and *Johannes Climacus*
PJS	*Papers and Journals: A Selection*
PV	*The Point of View for My Work as an Author*
SLW	*Stages on Life's Way*
SuD	*The Sickness unto Death*
TA	*Two Ages: The Age of Revolution and The Present Age*
DIO	*Three Discourses on Imagined Occasions*
UDVS	*Upbuilding Discourse in Various Spirits*
WoL	*Works of Love*

CHAPTER 1

INTRODUCTION, HISTORICAL CONTEXT AND BIOGRAPHICAL OUTLINE

i. SHORT INTRODUCTION: A STARTING PLACE FOR KIERKEGAARD

It is at Kierkegaard's insights into the difficulties and sorrows of this life that many of his readers will have started with him. Beginning with Kierkegaard in that way can work very well, whether our interest in Kierkegaard is just scholarly, or whether we are looking to Kierkegaard for wisdom that will help us to lead good lives, or both. Those sorts of insights can, for example, be found among the 'Diapsalmata' in the first part of *Either/Or* (*Enten–Eller*), in *Repetition* (*Gjentagelsen*) and in *Stages on Life's Way* (*Stadier paa Livets Vei*). As our reading of Kierkegaard continues, though, we may become just as interested in what he thinks could follow the contemplation of sorrow and hardship, or in his thoughts about what can be constructed from the sorrow and hardship. We may even consider that the thoughts on what might follow – encounters with or contemplation of the hardship – could be an equally good place to start for newcomers to the works of Kierkegaard.

At any rate, the question of where to start with philosophy was, interestingly enough, one that preoccupied him a great deal, as is shown by the little piece telling the story of the young Johannes Climacus, 'De Omnibus Dubitandum Est' (posthumously published under various titles, including simply: *Johannes Climacus*) and the associated entries in Kierkegaard's journals. Hegel's attempt to start with nothing – which will become such a familiar point of reference for readers of Kierkegaard – makes an appearance, rather fittingly perhaps, on the first page of one of the Dane's earliest publications, *From the Papers of One Still Living* (*Af en endnu Levendes Papirer*).

Furthermore, questions about the correct starting place for specific processes in thought, or movements of the soul, are frequently embedded in the discussions of those processes and movements, so that, for example, in 'On the Occasion of a Confession' we have the following passage (and the implication here is that the discourse upon confession will trace out the order of events in the life of the one confessing):

> So now the discourse stands at the beginning. This does not happen through wonder, but truly not through doubt either, because the person who doubts his guilt is only making a bad beginning, or rather he is continuing what was badly begun with sin. (DIO 29)

If the insights into life's difficulties and sorrows are to be a possible starting place for some, then it is as well to say now that there are no cosmic or quasi-mystical justifications for the suffering of the world in Kierkegaard. Still less is there any turning away from the reality of suffering. Kierkegaard's dialectical transformations of hardship into something that can move a person forward and outward – see especially his *Christian Discourses* (*Christelige Taler*) – are not proffered as answers to the problem of evil. However, what we do find in Kierkegaard, and especially in his edifying or 'upbuilding' works, is a way of thinking that may help us each to create a better world within ourselves. But this does not have to pave the way for those brands of individualism that do not give a hang for anybody else, as the investigations of Alastair Hannay – which we will come to in Chapter 6 – will show. Creating a better world within ourselves (as Kierkegaard urges us to do with his concept of 'self-activity') does not mean creating a better world only *for* ourselves.

Kierkegaard stands out in the nineteenth century as a Christian philosopher who starts with human beings as they are in the here-and-now. As George Pattison has noted, the aesthetic parts of his authorship were needed, Kierkegaard believed, because of the aesthetic nature of his age. According to Pattison:

> Kierkegaard is not just saying, 'I, because of my own particular way to Christianity through an aesthetically misspent youth, have chosen to concern myself with that particular form of moral and religious deviancy that finds its epitome in the fevered production and excessive enjoyment of works of art to the

> detriment of practical and spiritual life—I leave it to others differently qualified to deal with the many other forms of moral and religious sickness to be found amongst us (philistinism, nationalism, vice or whatever).'[1]

As well as the edifying or 'upbuilding' discourses, then, we have the dazzling, witty and often deeply dialectical thought-experiments of the pseudonymous authorship whose accomplishment has been, at least partly, to have entertained readers. This fitted with an idea that a teacher (perhaps especially a teacher who repeatedly professes to be 'without authority') should meet the learner wherever the learner currently resides. This is not to say that there is nothing gentle or enticing about the signed works of edification, nor is it to claim that the pseudonyms are all examples of Kierkegaard stooping to make allowances; Anti-Climacus (a character whom Kierkegaard places 'higher' than himself in terms of closeness to the requirement of Christianity) and Vigilius Haufniensis are arguably less ready to parley with the above-mentioned contemporary age and its aesthetic orientation than Søren Kierkegaard himself was, at least as he appears in, say, *Works of Love* (*Kjerlighedens Gjerninger*), or *Three Discourses for Imagined Occasions* (*Tre Taler ved tænkte Leiligheder*).

At any rate, the starting point for Kierkegaard in his bid to refresh the meaning of Christianity was not a premise, a foundation or a proof, but a human being. Kierkegaard's human being is already caught up in life, quickly distracted and easily led. So this is where Kierkegaard starts: with the human being he hopes will come to resist all these distractions and become a 'single individual', since individuality in Kierkegaard is importantly what subjectivity gains at the moment it ceases merely to observe. Reminding us, at least in this respect, of Blaise Pascal (1623–1662), Kierkegaard's aim was to go and find the human beings *where they were* – in the thick of immediacy – and start there. For this reason he published pseudonymous works on romantic themes and invented characters that would sing the praises of sensuality, and even elevate to the status of an art-form the cultivation *of* sensuality. Examples include the banquet ('In Vino Veritas') in *Stages on Life's Way*, 'Crop Rotation' in *Either/Or* and the reflections of *Writing Sampler*.

Kierkegaard does look at other ways to start. For example, in that short work *Johannes Climacus* ('De omnibus dubitandum est' is now usually given as the subtitle), we have a report on the adventures of a young philosopher who takes to heart the teaching of speculative philosophy that philosophy should have a 'presuppositionless' beginning, that it should start by doubting everything, the teaching that it should start, indeed, with absolutely nothing.[2] But philosophy does not start with absolutely nothing in Kierkegaard. Philosophy does not start with doubt in Kierkegaard, as it does for Descartes. Nor does philosophy start with wonder in Kierkegaard, as it had done for Aristotle, nor with suffering as it had done for Schopenhauer. Moreover, as far as Kierkegaard is concerned, philosophy does not start with any such encounter with the objective. The Dane displaces all such encounters and all questions about existence with a question about how to exist. Indeed, all the above ways to start with philosophy can be said to belong to the aesthetic outlook if we are taking up Kierkegaard's broader but also more profound conception of the aesthetic. That is to say, if by 'the aesthetic' we understand not just the contemplation, refined or otherwise, of either art itself or of what is thought artistic in life, but also the mindset of a whole age. This mindset, whether or not it cares for Mozart's *Don Giovanni*, would be aesthetic according to Kierkegaard because it is the mindset of just watching, absorbing and witnessing, and of *mere knowing*. This mindset is highly attractive – for Kierkegaard himself as well as for the dandies, the ordinary folk and the philosophy professors – because of its 'timelessness'. In our times, radio and television would count as 'the aesthetic' in Kierkegaard's deeper and broader sense, even if we are not listening to or watching a programme about fine art, because of our 'timeless' observation. And a very tempting timelessness it is too, at the end of a long week.

In contrast with 'the aesthetic' understood in this way, we have 'the existential'; the realm in which we become deciders, agents and thus willing (or reluctant) embracers of time. Decision-making is often associated with bravery. This is understandable, because when we decide a thing we are facing up to the reality of time and also, perhaps, to the irreversibility of what it will now contain. The transformation of questions about life into questions about how to live, of questions about existence into questions about ways to exist and, essentially, of objective issues into subjective ones occurs everywhere in Kierkegaard. Of all the philosophers, Kierkegaard has perhaps most often been associated with anguish and despair and we will be looking at despair in Chapter 5. This reputation notwithstanding, it will be seen that the reactions in his journals to the lectures he attended and to the books he studied are full of life and vigour. The search for help with the existential questions often crops up, especially the ones that did not seem to have been addressed by the greatest philosopher of that era, G. W. F. Hegel (1770–1831), about whose effect on Kierkegaard we should say more.

Although Kierkegaard accepted the vocabulary of Hegel's highly popular speculative philosophy into his own work to a degree – we encounter it especially in his dissertation *The Concept of Irony with Continual Reference to Socrates* (*Om Begrebet Ironi med stadigt Hensyn til Socrates*) – Kierkegaard was always reacting against Hegelianism. Subjectivity in Hegel's *Phenomenology of Spirit* (*Phänomenologie des Geistes*) is *all of mind everywhere*; all the apprehending that occurs on the way to Spirit's realization of itself. Kierkegaardian subjectivity, in striking contrast, is an issue that each must face alone. Subjectivity in Hegel is objectively described as an entity in the universe, while in Kierkegaard, fittingly enough, it is passionately addressed in the reader. Any objective descriptions of subjectivity in Kierkegaard have a satirical flavour, notably those of Johannes Climacus in *Concluding Unscientific Postscript to* Philosophical Fragments (*Afsluttende Uvidenskabelig Efterskrift til de* Philosophiske Smuler).

Now, aside from all Kierkegaard's provocative experimentation with Hegelian language, there was certainly going to be a serious problem with Hegel for Kierkegaard. It is one that we can characterize in a fairly formal way with reference to what we have said so far: the prime issue for Hegel was knowledge, with all forms of human activity having their special place as 'moments' in the self-knowledge of Absolute Spirit, and even religion being accorded a position of truth – yes – but truth in the form of a 'picture-thinking' moment, ultimately subordinate to pure knowledge. This may be related to Hegel's view of sin – a concept we will discuss later on – as merely 'negative'.[3] In a sense then, we can present Kierkegaard's well-known difference from Hegel in terms of Hegelian philosophy's refusal, or supposed refusal, to exist outside 'the aesthetic' or to transcend the narrated history of subjectivity's developing apprehension of all things. That said, Hegel appears to have laid down something that existentialism would be able to pick up when he writes:

> In the present, morality is assumed as *already in existence*, and actuality is so placed that it is not in harmony with it. The *actual*

> moral consciousness, however, is one that *acts*; it is precisely therein that the actuality of its morality consists.[4]

Stephen D. Crites, in the introduction to his translation of Kierkegaard's *The Crisis and a Crisis in the Life of an Actress* (*Krisen og en Krise i en Skuespillerindes Liv*), writes:

> Kierkegaard's preoccupation with the distinction between the aesthetic and the existential was not aroused simply by what seemed to be the confusion of the categories which had resulted from philosophical imperialism, however. In fact, he saw the attempt to accommodate existence to the standpoint of the philosophical spectator as simply a grandiose projection of a way of life prevalent in the modern world.[5]

Of course, it could also be shown that Hegel's position precisely did not reflect, nor embody, certain post-enlightenment tendencies, and specifically the value placed upon reasoning things out for oneself. This is something that in *Elements of the Philosophy of Right* (*Grundlinien der Philosophie des Rechts*) is reckoned by Hegel to be a potential menace to the harmony of the Universal as represented by the State. Nevertheless, it was this idea of the Universal and specifically the notion that Christianity could be made completely welcome and could feel absolutely at home within that Universal (as manifested in the State) that exercised Kierkegaard. The philosophical subsuming of Christianity into the System was a condescension which could be seen as lining up all too readily with the blithe complacency of taking oneself to be Christian on the basis that one has, after all, been born in Denmark.[6]

Kierkegaard was having none of it. He was a nimble dialectician, a vigorous polemicist, and an ardent campaigner for a decidedly truer and deeper Christianity than the sort he saw as being prevalent in Denmark in the 1840s and 1850s. Just as Socrates invited people to explore the key moral categories governing their judgements and perceptions, so Kierkegaard invited his readers to become single individuals who might reintroduce Christianity into Christendom.

ii. BIOGRAPHICAL OUTLINE

Søren Aabye Kierkegaard was born in Copenhagen on 5 May 1813 (a year of economic crisis in Denmark in which, as Kierkegaard liked to point out, many a bad banknote was put into circulation). He was the youngest of seven children. His father, Michael Pedersen Kierkegaard (1756–1838), was born the son of Jutland peasants and started out as a shepherd boy on the heaths. In that occupation he was on one occasion so tormented by the harshness of the elements that he stood upon a hill and apparently spoke curses against God. The memory of this rebellion was the source, in Søren's view, of his father's 'silent despair'; at any rate, Michael Pedersen was still haunted by it at the very end of his life according to Søren's account. Conclusions may be drawn from the mention made by pseudonymous author Vigilius Haufniensis in *The Concept of Anxiety* (*Begrebet Angest*) of 'the way a child wishes to be guilty along with the father' (CA 29). While still a youngster, Michael Pedersen had then set off for Copenhagen where he was to make his fortune as a draper. Indeed, he performed so well in this trade that he was able to sell the business as early as 1786 in order to pursue the study of theology, assisted in this by his friend (and later the primate of the Danish State Church), Bishop J. P. Mynster.

Søren's mother, Ane Sørensdatter Lund Kierkegaard, had been a maid in the household before marrying Michael Pedersen who had lost his first wife, Kirstine Røyen Kierkegaard, after only two years of marriage. The lovers Ane and Michael had been intimate outside of wedlock not so long after the latter had become a widower. It is widely thought that guilt associated with this, and with the resulting pregnancy, compounded Michael Pedersen's belief that there was a curse upon the family and, later, that the loss of five children out of the seven born to the couple amounted to a divine punishment. In 1819, Søren's brother, Søren Michael, died following an accident in a playground, and three years later his sister Maren Kirstine was also to die. Ane had been forty-five when Søren was born, Michael Pedersen fifty-seven. Søren lost his mother, believed to have been the calming influence in the Kierkegaard household, in 1834. Julia Watkin takes note in her 'Historical Introduction' to *Early Polemical Writings* of a recounting (in H. L. Martensen's *Af mit Levnet* by his own mother) of the extreme distress into which Kierkegaard was plunged by the loss of his mother (*EPW* xvi–xvii). 1834 is also the year in which Kierkegaard loses the last of his sisters, Petrea. Kierkegaard begins to keep a journal in this year.

Søren's brother, Peter Christian Kierkegaard (1805–1888), was a politician and a theologian and was Bishop of Aalborg from 1857 to 1875. Peter Christian sometimes criticized his brother's works (for example at the Roskilde Ecclesiastical Conventions in 1849 and 1855) expressing particular discomfort with the 'infinite requirement' referred to in the pseudonymous authorship,[7] but he delivered the eulogy at his brother's funeral. A nephew of Søren, one Henrik Sigvard Lund, who protested at Kierkegaard's burial service that his uncle's dying wishes were not being observed, was the son of Kierkegaard's sister Nicoline Christine. Nicoline died in 1832, ten years after the death of Maren Kirstine. Niels Andreas would die in America the following year.

Søren Kierkegaard's father died in August 1838 aged 82. In the March of that year, Kierkegaard had also lost his dear friend Paul Martin Møller. Before leaving this world, Michael Pedersen is supposed to have asked that Søren complete his education in theology at the University of Copenhagen.[8] In previous years Søren had found it hard to settle to his work, but had become determined to read for his finals in the months leading up to his father's death. Following that awful and momentous event, Kierkegaard considered it imperative, for the sake of his father's memory, that he study for the theological examination. He engaged the help of a private tutor, Hans Brøchner, at this time. In 1841 Kierkegaard was awarded the degree of *magister artium* (equivalent to a Ph.D. today, and officially recognized in Denmark as a doctoral degree in 1854) for the work that would be published as *The Concept of Irony with continual reference to Socrates*. Kierkegaard's proficiency in Latin was indisputable, he having taught Latin in the mid-to-late 1830s in order to assist his friend Professor Nielsen at the Borgerdyds School (at which Kierkegaard himself had been enrolled as a youngster in 1821). However, Kierkegaard petitioned the King of Denmark in June for permission to submit the dissertation in Danish.[9] His public defence of that dissertation took place at the end of September 1841.

Regine Olsen (1822–1904), the daughter of a Copenhagen dignitary, was the love of Kierkegaard's life. Søren and Regine were to form a bond as soon as they met on 8 May 1837. On 8 September 1840, Kierkegaard formally proposed to Regine and she accepted his offer, but in August of the following year Kierkegaard felt unable to go forward with the arrangement. He therefore 'broke it off'; his thought that a strong tendency towards melancholia made him unfit for marriage has not always been taken to offer the full explanation by commentators and critics. In *Prefaces* (*Forord*), the pseudonymous author Nicolas Notabene depicts marriage as a conflicting responsibility in respect of his aspirations to become a writer[10] and it is not impossible Kierkegaard had had those kinds of thoughts about his own situation in 1841. However, a genuine fear that aspects of his personality and temperament would have made him a terrible burden to his potential partner was almost certainly a major factor. That Kierkegaard, recognizing the possible problems, may have been prepared to act accordingly, and in a principled way, seems plausible enough as an explanation, albeit an incomplete one. At any rate, there is no reason to rule out this interpretation of his decision to end the engagement. It is also possible that Kierkegaard's inheritance, while being sufficient to support him in his own life as an author, would not have been sufficient for the support of Regine and any children that may have been born to them. The question 'Why then does Abraham do it?' – asked by Johannes de Silentio in Kierkegaard's *Fear and Trembling* (*Frygt og Bæven*) (FT/R 59), a work whose subject (the story of the possible sacrifice of Isaac) is thought to have been selected by Kierkegaard as providing an analogue to the sacrifice he had made in his own life – is one that has been asked by commentators and historians of ideas ever since, only with the name 'Kierkegaard' being substituted for 'Abraham'.

Instead of her Søren, then, Regine would marry another. Her husband was to be one Johan Frederik Schlegel (1817–1896), a prominent civil servant – not to be confused with the philosopher Friedrich von Schlegel (1772–1829), author of *Lucinde* and a leading figure in German Romanticism. In his essay, 'The Wound of Negativity: Two Kierkegaardian Texts', George Steiner provides us with a strong and telling evocation of Kierkegaard's reaction to the news of this new engagement of Regine to J. F. Schlegel:

> The psychological effect was both ruinous and liberating. Wild energies of argumentative, allegoric self-dramatization and social satire erupted in Kierkegaard. His henceforth aloneness turned to strategy. He took his stance at the frontiers of his community and of his own psyche.[11]

Despite everything, Regine and her husband maintained a close interest in the work of Søren Kierkegaard – it is said that they would read it to one another – but Schlegel did not agree to a request from Søren for a meeting with Regine.

At the end of 1845, an article published by one Peder Ludvig Møller – most definitely not to be confused with Poul Martin Møller, a close friend of Kierkegaard's to whom we shall come shortly – was to set in motion a chain of events that would bring much unhappiness to Kierkegaard. This article by Peder Ludvig Møller, who had studied at the University of Copenhagen at the same time as Kierkegaard, contained indirect criticism of *Stages on Life's Way*. Entitled 'A Visit in Sorø' it appeared at the end of 1845 in a yearbook started by Møller himself, *Gæa*. It paid Kierkegaard some compliments while raising a question as to whether he was capable of directing his talents into something more coherent.

Now Peder Ludvig Møller was a contributor to and some-time editor of *The Corsair*, a satirical magazine that specialized in producing caricatures of prominent figures in public life and lampooning their behaviour, or alleged behaviour. Kierkegaard's response to Møller, published in the newspaper *Fædrelandet* (*The Fatherland*) just after Christmas, 1845, was 'The Activity of a Traveling Esthetician and How He Still Happened to Pay for the Dinner'. This little piece was full of sarcasm, and in it Peder Ludvig Møller was portrayed as indulging in a facile attempt to impress the literati of Copenhagen. In an arguably quite ill-advised subsequent piece entitled 'Dialectical Result of a Literary Police Action', Kierkegaard, writing under the pseudonym Frater Taciturnus, maintained that to be immortalized in a paper like *The Corsair* would actually be a personal injury and that he would therefore prefer to be made the subject of its abuse (COR 47, 50) which, alas, he then duly was.

Although Kierkegaard would reason in his journals that the resulting unpleasantness was in some ways pivotal in helping to determine some important life-decisions (he abandoned a plan to enter the Church, or possibly to become a teacher; what is referred to occasionally in the literature as Kierkegaard's 'Second Authorship'[12] is considered to have started at this point), the whole affair was terribly unfortunate. Kierkegaard became the target of what amounted to playground bullying in the street (this included mockery of his clothes and his posture), and this caused him to abandon the walks around Copenhagen that had thitherto been such a great source of inspiration to him.

In the final phase of his life, and in what could be thought of as the third phase of his authorship, Kierkegaard shifted his whole approach to writing quite decisively away from what he had called 'the indirect communication', a move that is signaled even in the titles chosen for the pieces from this period, such as, for example: *This Must Be Said; So Let It Be Said* (*Dette skal siges; saa være det da sagt*). The move to direct (and, perhaps regrettably, less dialectical) communication was occasioned by the death of the Bishop Primate of the Danish People's Church, J. P. Mynster, at the start of 1854. Mynster had been a friend and pastor to the Kierkegaard family and a person for whom Søren had had much fondness and respect. Nevertheless, Kierkegaard was greatly annoyed by a pronouncement from the new Bishop Primate elect, H. L. Martensen, that the departed Mynster had been 'a witness to the truth'. Kierkegaard began a prolonged attack on the established church of Denmark in the newspaper *Fædrelandet* (*The Fatherland*), and by means of a broadsheet called *The Moment* (*Øieblikket*) – also translated as *The Instant*. We will be discussing this part of Kierkegaard's authorship towards the end of this book. On 28 September 1855 Kierkegaard collapsed in the street. He was carrying the last number of *The Moment*. A few days later he was admitted to Frederiksberg Hospital in Copenhagen, where he died on 11 November.

In Kierkegaard's dying days he let it be known to his friend Emil Boesen that he would only receive the Eucharist if it were to be administered by a layperson. Bruce H. Kirmmse notes that Søren's brother, the pastor Peter Christian Kierkegaard, had travelled from his parish at Pedersborg-by-Sorø in west-central Zealand (quite a way in those days) to visit his brother but, alas, was refused admission.[13]

iii. INFLUENCES AND HISTORICAL CONTEXT

Upheavals in Europe were frequent and widespread in Kierkegaard's time and the repercussions of these were often felt by Danes. Julia Watkin mentions (*EPW* viii) that Søren's brother, Peter Christian, happened to be staying in Paris at the time of the July Revolution in 1830 and actually ended up having to assist in the construction of barricades.[14] In Denmark, Frederik VI (1768–1839), who had himself taken power (by force but without bloodshed) in 1784 from his father, Christian VII (1749–1808), became increasingly concerned about his position over the years, notwithstanding the decline – caused by the pointless execution in France of Louis XVI in 1793 – in the popular support for the idea of revolution that had existed after 1789.

Frederik's concerns about the possibility of significant unrest in Denmark may have been unnecessary, however. Often visible in public spaces, and closely involved with Denmark's day-to-day affairs, he was held in considerable affection by his subjects. Watkin reports that it was quite common for the royal family to be seen being rowed along the canal in the palace gardens at Fredriksberg, 'watched by the Sunday afternoon crowds who were permitted to enjoy the gardens', and that 'if a fire broke out in the city at night, the King could be seen personally directing the fire-fighting operations' (*EPW* x). There had been serious fires in Copenhagen in 1794 and 1795.

Despite being in many ways a progressive ruler, and one who had managed to survive a series of crises – Watkin mentions Denmark's 'unwilling involvement in the Napoleonic wars with the loss of the fleet and the bombardment of Copenhagen by the English in 1807' as well as the national bankruptcy of 1813 and the loss of Norway in 1814 – Frederik was no forward-thinker when it came to freedom of the press. Infringement of press restrictions could lead to exile and did so in a number of cases. Some devolvement of power occurred in the early 1830s with the creation of Provincial Consultative Assemblies, but Frederik's acceptance of free expression in those arenas was not matched by a belief in the validity of criticisms aimed at the political establishment in the newspapers. It could be that Kierkegaard's 'render-unto-Caesar' attitude towards prevailing expectations and existing conditions is an index of the closed nature of the society in which he grew up.[15] However, it is equally possible that Kierkegaard – who felt that freedom of thought was more important than freedom of speech – saw the excitement of attempts to challenge the order of things as a distraction from a deeper contemplation of the human predicament.

Not a great deal of contemplation of the human predicament is required, however, for us to bear in mind that in the second half of the 1840s and the early 1850s European history shows us human suffering on an unimaginable scale in the shape of the Irish potato famine, also known as 'The Great Hunger'. In this period the population of Ireland was reduced by about a quarter. Approximately one million people emigrated and an estimated one million people perished in the most awful conditions. Although the immediate cause of the mass starvation is known to have been the potato blight (*phytophthora infestans*) which reduced the 1845 harvest by about half and which destroyed three-quarters of the crop in 1846, it is widely acknowledged that the size of the death-toll and the overall extent of the suffering can be attributed in part to the inherently exploitative conditions in which the majority of Ireland's rural population existed, and then also to the mishandling of the crisis by the British government. The famine was viewed by some of those in a position to offer the radical solutions necessary as a *dispensation of providence* and even as a kind of learning experience for the nation as a whole, an attitude which will strike most people now as callous in the extreme, to say the least.

In some ways it seems dreadfully ironic that elsewhere in Europe during the period of this indescribable misery there should have been a philosopher who was at pains to encourage individuals to look inward in order to *help themselves*. However, it should be noted that Kierkegaard did not expect anybody to look inward in order to uncover *the source* of all pain, but rather to look inward to uncover whatever resources may *counteract* that pain *whatever its source*. Moreover, we cannot say for sure that if those who were not being crushed by starvation (or by the often equally horrific alternatives to starvation laid on by the administration, such as workhouses or pointless labour-projects) had encountered and properly appropriated the teaching of, say, *Works of Love*,[16] they would not have felt compelled to act energetically to alleviate the sufferings of the undeniably helpless. We might also suspect, and indeed it is germane to this last point, that the Kierkegaardian idea that each one of us *can act within ourselves* concerns the battle against what are precisely the *internal* obstacles to becoming energetic, braver, more noble and more generous. Finally, on this topic, it should be noted that although Kierkegaard is often regarded as a conservative, he did not remain resistant to the case for better political representation. Bruce Kirmmse:

> Kierkegaard [. . .], despite a great many misgivings, eventually came to see the new democratic age as the inevitable way of the future and, indeed, as the will of '[Divine] Guidance' (*Styrelsen*). He came, for example, to see the atomism of the new age as fraught not merely with danger but also with the opportunity of developing each person into a full and responsible individual. In this, he differed greatly from the authority figures of the conservative mainstream of the Golden age, the men who had once been his mentors.[17]

We will be coming back to the important questions about Kierkegaard's different conceptions of society in the final chapter. But now let us turn to some of the literature that affected Kierkegaard and shaped his development.

Kierkegaard was influenced by quite a number of thinkers in his formative years, including Poul Martin Møller (1794–1838), Hamann (1730–1788), Schleiermacher (1768–1834), Schlegel (1772–1829), Sibbern (1785–1872), Heiberg (1791–1860), Lessing (1729–1781) and Trendelenberg (1802–1872). Kierkegaard was, to start with, very taken with the philosophy of Schelling (1775–1854), and he is, of course, well-known for having extensively criticized the speculative logic of G. W. F. Hegel (1770–1831). As Paul Ricouer has put it:

> Everybody knows that Kierkegaard was an anti-Hegelian. He said so himself. In fact he hardly said anything else.[18]

Kierkegaard often refers to Spinoza, and T. H. Croxall notes that he possessed all of Spinoza's works although, as Croxall observes, the impact of Spinoza's conception of the universe seems to have been limited.[19] Towards the end of his life, Kierkegaard came to the work of Arthur Schopenhauer (1788–1860), a philosopher with whom he felt considerable affinity, major differences on key points notwithstanding. Schopenhauer, though, was no dialectician, whereas Kierkegaard (aside, perhaps, from the very strident and sometimes quite brittle pronouncements of his very last writings) can really be regarded as dialectical through and through.

Professor Poul Martin Møller, poet, admirer of Socrates and author of a treatise on the topic of immortality (in which the conceptions of Fichte and Hegel, among others, are criticized), was a great influence upon and an inspiration to the young Kierkegaard, who would later dedicate *The Concept of Anxiety* to his memory. Møller is credited with having kept the young Kierkegaard on track, encouraging him to focus his talents and reign in his tendency to be polemical at every turn. It is even reckoned that Møller may have been the model – at least in that respect – for the character of Judge Wilhelm, whose letters to an aesthete make up the 'Papers of B' in *Either/Or* and who also appears in *Stages on Life's Way*. Møller died in 1838, the same year in which Søren had lost his father.

Immanuel Kant is likely to be thought of first when there is mention of a Königsberg philosopher but we also have Johann Georg Hamann, who was greatly admired by Kierkegaard. (Kant did in fact assist Hamann in securing employment in the tax office.) Also esteemed by the likes of Goethe and Hegel, J. G. Hamann, whose publications include *Brocken* (*Fragments*), developed imaginary personalities in order to explore various intellectual viewpoints, just as Kierkegaard was later to do with his marvellous array of pseudonymous authors. Moreover, scholars like T. H. Croxall consider that the influence of Hamann, whose own conversion had been decisive and dramatic,[20] and whose works Kierkegaard had encountered in the winter of 1835, was powerful in turning Kierkegaard back to Christianity.[21] The 'dialectical lyric' of Kierkegaard's *Fear and Trembling* begins with a quotation from Hamann.

Until his death in 1834, the German theologian Friedrich Daniel Ernst Schleiermacher was Professor of Theology at the Friedrich-Wilhelm University of Berlin, which Kierkegaard would later visit. In *On Religion: Speeches to its Cultural Despisers* (1799), Schleiermacher had sought to establish a clear separation between religion as that which is to be grasped by a faculty of *feeling*, and philosophy which is to be grasped by a faculty of cognition. Schleiermacher caused excitement when he visited Copenhagen in the September of 1833. It would appear that Schleiermacher's review of Friedrich von Schlegel's *Lucinde* had an impact on Kierkegaard's artistic method. In October of 1835, Kierkegaard notes that he has been reading this review, in which various viewpoints are expressed in the voices of different characters. On the philosophical and theological side of things, moreover, Kierkegaard had been introduced as a student to Schleiermacher's *Christian Faith* by his tutor Martensen. With his strong emphasis upon religious *feeling*, and also upon the value of wonder and humility, in contrast to religious faith as understood by Hegel,[22] we can see how Schleiermacher would have been attractive to the young Kierkegaard. Nevertheless, for Schleiermacher – and in this he does resemble Hegel – it was acceptable for religion to take the form of a sort of climate, or other such naturally arising condition. Kierkegaard might have understood only too well what Schleiermacher meant, but he would not have considered it acceptable.

It is also easy to see how Lessing, with his emphasis (following Socrates and Michel de Montaigne) on the importance of self-examination as a pre-requisite for any journey towards important truths, would have appealed to Kierkegaard. Lessing's notion of truth as subjectivity surfaces in Kierkegaard's thinking, especially in Johannes Climacus's *Concluding Unscientific Postscript to* Philosophical Fragments, which also includes explicit and extensive discussion of Lessing.

Kierkegaard was drawn to Berlin by the lectures of Friedrich Wilhelm Joseph von Schelling, who opposed many of Hegel's ideas, though the two had been friends at university. The notes that Kierkegaard took from Schelling's lectures are in the Royal Library in Copenhagen. These Schelling lectures were also attended by such eminent figures as Karl Marx (1818–1883) and Jacob Burckhardt (1818–1897). Journal entries from 1841 show that Kierkegaard was at first enchanted and enthused by Schelling's philosophy. Part of the appeal of that philosophy for a thinker such as Kierkegaard was going to be the view that rational enquiry alone could not lead consciousness to a complete apprehension of reality as envisaged in the Hegelian idea of the Absolute. For all Kierkegaard's eventual exasperation with Schelling,[23] it could be that the Dane's objection to any summary (and Hegelian summaries especially) of existence as knowledge-in-waiting was nourished in part by Schelling's criticisms of Hegel.

The poet, playwright, philosopher, some-time director of The Royal Theatre in Copenhagen, and author of *On the Significance of Philosophy for the Present Age* (*Om Philosophiens Betydning for den nuværende Tid*), Johan Ludvig Heiberg (1791–1860) is a key figure in the Kierkegaard story. J. L. Heiberg, who came to be recognized as the arbiter of quality in Danish literature, especially in the 1830s, was the son of the political writer Peter Andreas Heiberg and Thomasine Christine Gyllembourg, later Baroness Gyllembourg-Ehrensvärd (1773–1856). Kierkegaard's writings include enthusiastic responses to novels by Heiberg's mother. See, for example *Two Ages: A Literary Review* (*En literair Anmeldelse*) and also *From the Papers of One Still Living* (*Af en endnu Levendes Papirer*), in which Gyllembourg's *A Story of Everyday Life* (*En Hverdags-Historie*) is favourably compared to *Only a Fiddler* (*Kun en Spillemand*) by Hans Christian Andersen. Much later on, using the pseudonym Inter et Inter, Kierkegaard also responded to the art of Heiberg's wife, a highly regarded actress, Johanne Luise Heiberg (née Pätges) (1812–1890); see *The Crisis and A Crisis in the Life of an Actress* (already mentioned above). Heiberg's endorsement of Hegel's philosophy is considered to have contributed significantly to the growth of Denmark's interest in Hegel.

From 1827 to 1830 Heiberg edited *The Flying Post* (*Flyvende Post*), a popular weekly at which Kierkegaard did occasionally poke fun; see, for example, Nicolas Notabene's *Prefaces*, in which there is also a fair deal of lively satire directed at a gilt-edged and copiously ornamented publication of Heiberg's entitled *Urania: Yearbook for 1844*. However, Heiberg is thought ultimately to have taken Kierkegaard's teasing in good sport[24] and did not omit Notabene's *Prefaces* from the collection of Kierkegaard's works he was eventually to edit. More generally, Heiberg must have regarded with relative equanimity the fairly mordant satire directed at him personally by Kierkegaard, both in *Prefaces* and *Concluding Unscientific Postscript to* Philosophical Fragments. Some of these gibes came as a consequence, perhaps, of the review Heiberg wrote of *Either/Or*.

In addition to books of philosophy, Kierkegaard's library contained much in the way of poetry, drama and other writing. Croxall mentions Danish works by Baggesen and Øehlenschläger (whom P. L. Møller had hoped to succeed as professor of aesthetics at the University of Copenhagen), and works in German by Tieck, Novalis, Brentano, Kleist, Schiller, Heine and others. Kierkegaard often makes use of Shakespeare whose works he had come to know, at least in part, through Tieck's translations.

Above all, however, Kierkegaard took his inspiration from The Holy Bible. It was always to the Scriptures that he turned when, in order to accompany what he was holding out to us in his left hand, that is to say, a pseudonymous work, with the offer of something in his right hand, he would compose a work that would bear his own name. A great deal of attention has been paid to the pseudonymous authorship and a vast amount of exciting and illuminating research exists to help us understand the rich and colourful world that Kierkegaard created in it. So often, however, when critics and commentators feel the need to break off from the task of interpreting the pseudonyms and look for what Kierkegaard himself *really thought* (for want of a better phrase) they will turn to Kierkegaard's *Journals and Papers*. To be sure, there may be a time and a place for doing that, especially since the *Journals and Papers* obviously contain many revealing and instructive passages.[25] But they also contain – as is quite natural – much that is half-formed and experimental. There are also some responses to events that do not seem to be very dialectical (at least by the standards of a writer who is, after all, one of the most dialectical thinkers who ever lived), as well as a number of passages that perhaps are not altogether worthy of Søren Kierkegaard. Among the later journal entries,[26] for example, there are writings that lack the intimacy, warmth and generosity of, say, the edifying works of the mid-1840s, as well as one or two remarks that reveal him to be, as the saying goes, *human, all too human* – not that he ever claimed to be anything else.

So perhaps, when we want access to something that might be close to *what Kierkegaard really thought* – whatever it might mean for anyone really to think anything[27] – why not start with the edifying works authored by one S. Kierkegaard? In *Starting with Kierkegaard*, we will try to do this as much as possible, notwithstanding the possibility that 'S. Kierkegaard' may have occasionally been a kind of pseudonym. The edifying is nothing to be afraid of, after all. In so many ways it can come to the rescue when we are trying to read for the real Kierkegaard, and, for all those who may be interested, it can also come to the rescue in real life.

CHAPTER 2

CENTRAL THEMES AND KEY MOTIFS

i. THE OCCASION AND AN OCCASION FOR STARTING

Across the pseudonymous authorship, and in the signed works also, we are sure to run into Kierkegaard's bemusement at the idea of our ever being able to see one event as the certain consequence of another. He is terribly puzzled by this idea. He also accepts it as part of life. But really, he replaces the idea with the pathos of a hope, not to say the pathos of an implicitly vain hope. This is all brought into focus by Kierkegaard's attention to something called *the occasion* (*Anledning*) and we will shortly look at this 'occasion' as it appears in *Either/Or* (*Enten–Eller*). 'The occasion' in Kierkegaard represents an earnestness about getting to the bottom of explanations that prevents the dialectical process of dismantling them from turning into a mere exercise. Nor does the approach degenerate into simply scoffing at the explanations *of others*; the Socratic doggedness of Kierkegaard's 'occasion' is applied to all particular causal explanations, not just some explanations in particular.

Along with his breezy scepticism in the face of all explanation and all attribution of supposed effects *in the world as such*, we have Kierkegaard's smilingly experimental responses to the idea of special times for certain activities, be they traditionally enshrined special times, or the special times wished for by an individual soul. His irony in respect of the latter is the more palatable for being bound up with what seems to be a real wish for certain days to have special meaning and so on.

Kierkegaard's way of relating to the Church Calendar is both dialectical and subjunctive in character. Holy occasions are continually important to him and at the same time they are continually vanishing in his recognition that what the occasion contains and imparts must be taken away and recalled again and again when there is no occasion other than the occasion of inwardness itself. The externality retains all significance, however, because of our weakness. But to the extent that we can be strong it vanishes, and so here we see a dialectical movement. The subjunctive mood lives in relation to the Sacraments as embraced by Kierkegaard. '[T]he task is to remain at the Communion table when you leave the Communion table' (CDCLA 274) says Kierkegaard in the third of his *Discourses at the Communion on Fridays*. Truly to be at the Communion table, then, *includes* not being at the Communion table but being somewhere else *as if you were* at the Communion table. But there is something else to consider, aside from the dialectical and subjunctive appropriations of sacred externalities and occasions (that could so easily have been inimical to a free-thinker like Kierkegaard), and that is his interest in the external occasion that is slightly 'in the margins' or off the beaten track in respect of conventional practice. His attention to Friday Communion explicitly embodies and betokens this interest.

Being, as he never tires of saying, *without authority*, Kierkegaard writes discourses for special occasions – *imagined* special occasions – at which he will probably not be able to preside. Nor does there appear to be any strong certainty that the addressed listener to the discourse will have an occasion lined up on which these potential contributions could become *fully themselves* – by contributing at an appointed time.

> An unauthorized discourse, however, has no lovers to unite. But despite that, my listener, you can readily hear it. (DIO 45)

So, when calling on whichever hearer may be in that situation of lacking an occasion then to produce the appropriate conditions imaginatively, Kierkegaard ironizes not only the well-meant purposefulness of his offering (it should be easy to defend the creation of an occasion-based piece of writing), but also that perennial insistence on being without authority. For all the playfulness directed at the sort of occasional writing issued by a Heiberg, say, and notwithstanding any satirical allusions to the pomp or security of those in a position respectfully to present something or other on a special occasion, there is a kind of report on Kierkegaard's own exclusion in these writings, writings that practically confess at the outset that they have been occasioned only by the need for an occasion; there is also, perhaps, a melancholy remembrance of his own cancelled marriage. That Kierkegaard was without authority is interesting; that he lacked an occasion may, ironically enough, be pivotal. For just at the point when his yearning for an occasion resonates and is poignant, his persistence in writing for an occasion, despite lacking one, seems consonant with his influential and well-documented search (on behalf of all human beings) for something resembling self-determination.

Very poignant, and quite significant for grasping the spirit of Kierkegaard, is his encouragement of one who *does* happen to have an occasion, to appropriate it in such a way that she would have one – have one *for herself* – whether or not she had one in a merely actual way (as Kierkegaard might say). This is the Dane writing to his young niece Henriette Lund in 1843:

> My dear Jette, [. . .] Allow me to take this opportunity to congratulate you on your birthday, whether this congratulation now arrives about a year late or a few days early—for one really must not take life that seriously, nor is it granted to everybody, to me in particular, always to hit on what is right, especially in these matters. (LD 155–156)

We see here how Kierkegaard makes a point of being contentedly resigned to the uncertainty in a way that perhaps prefigures the 'approximation' that Johannes Climacus will ascribe to all merely human understanding in *Concluding Unscientific Postscript*. A paragraph or two later, Kierkegaard puts:

> May everything go well for you in the new year which you enter upon today—ignore dates and anniversaries and all such extraneous matters as I ignore them—today is your birthday. That is how I want it, and I am in charge here. If it is not your birthday today, then an error must have crept into your baptismal certificate, in which case you will have to have a serious talk with your father, since this is a serious matter in this serious world, in which, as experience teaches, even though one otherwise knew everything and were the very model of perfection, one would still be utterly useless if one did not know one's own birthday. (LD 158)

Later on in this book we will come to what Theodor W. Adorno sees as an 'indifferentiation of subject and object' in Kierkegaard.

Adorno's critique deserves consideration for all sorts of reasons. But if we might just pre-empt such consideration for a moment, we could observe in this letter to young Henriette a certain pathos: it is as if Kierkegaard knows that what may indeed be a sought-after indifferentiation of the sort Adorno describes must come back and collide with externality – with what Adorno himself might term *administered reality*. Kierkegaard is no solipsist; he makes fun of his own 'I am in charge here' when he recommends that his dear 'Jette' should take steps to have the external world rectified in accordance with an appropriation so radical that it would practically efface, or at least challenge, the very occasion whose meaning was to be appropriated. Subjunctivity, just when it asserts itself, appears as doomed, and indeed, Adorno himself would probably be quick to detect a little bit of sadness in Kierkegaard's laughter. But let us come back to the occasion in general.

In the first part of *Either/Or* we are treated to a charismatic improvisation on the strangeness of *the occasion* – which is there referred to as a 'category' – at the start of a discussion by 'A' of a one-act play by Scribe entitled *The First Love*, translated by Heiberg. This discussion provides us with a fine and sparkling lesson in how we could go about addressing some of the most dramatic issues of our existence in quite a nimble way. It is as if Kierkegaard is turning reflection upon what could count as causation into a kind of dance. Or, it is as if by being light-footed enough merely to dance around this problem he has found a means to step right inside it in a way that even a long treatise on causation might struggle to do.

Almost in passing, and before the discussion is fully underway, Kierkegaard's look at *the occasion* exposes absurdities in the sort of human reasoning that is most familiar to us – we are not dealing at this point with the absurdity of anything as momentous as, for example, human belief in the paradox of a God appearing in time – or at least it exposes a dizzying open-endedness in that familiar style of reasoning. When, for example, the occasion is described as the 'extra element' needed 'for an inner decision to become an outer decision' (EOI 233), this is, we might say, seriously in jest. The reasoning upon which the very notion of decision must be balanced now looks questionable. An 'outer decision' seems comical. And yet if there is never any graduation of a decision into the externality of what can be called action, then few would think the term 'decision' at all appropriate, assuming that the obstacles have not themselves been external.

So where exactly is *the decision*? Is it somehow stretched across the initial deliberation, the formulated aim, the actions undertaken and the recorded result? Or is it that 'decision' is ultimately nothing but a fondly cherished myth behind which reality contains nothing but a plain sequence of events, a sequence of events that does not include any separate deciding-event? If decision were going to be abolished as a concept, perhaps there would be some philosophers in favour. But if it is to be kept in service then the implication is that philosophy, and indeed thought itself, should not be deprived of this *other* piece of nonsense, *the occasion*, the at-once all-encompassing and completely unimportant *occasion*:

> So the occasion is simultaneously the most significant and the most insignificant, the highest and the lowest, the most important and the most unimportant. Without the occasion, nothing at all actually occurs, and yet the occasion has no part at all in what occurs. (EOI 238)

Logic – yes, the whole of logic – is explicitly charged (in this chatty little introduction to the review of *The First Love*!) with being unable to comprehend this mysterious and elusive occasion. The suggestion is that the occasion, as well as being essential to the start of something, is inherently ungraspable (and let us notice here the mention of paradox):

> In the idea, all actuality can be in readiness—without the occasion, it never becomes actual. The occasion is a finite category, and it is impossible for immanental thinking to grasp it; it is too much of a paradox for that. But for that reason the occasion is also the most amusing, the most interesting, the wittiest of all categories. Like a wren it is everywhere and nowhere. (EOI 238)

We have touched upon the theme of decision, and we have perhaps even pointed the way to the rational grounds for regarding decision as inevitably non-rational. But if we come back to the theme of causation, and to the question of how one event can be said to have started with another, we see that with this jokey and mischievous excursion, around the occasion, major problems have surfaced. These problems are in philosophy and, moreover, in language itself. We will see them highlighted again and again by Kierkegaard. The occasion is far from being the only non-logical broker or catalyst 'between' potential and accomplishment in Kierkegaardian discourse, as can be seen in *The Concept of Anxiety* (*Begrebet Angest*) when Vigilius Haufniensis tells us:

> In a logical system, it is convenient to say that possibility passes over into actuality. However, in actuality it is not so convenient, and an intermediate term is required. The intermediate term is anxiety, but it no more explains the qualitative leap than it can justify it ethically. (CA 49)

In ordinary parlance, even in quite formal ordinary parlance, we are used to hearing how something 'depends on the situation' and yet the meaning of 'situation' here is exhausted by being that upon which a thing will depend. 'Situation' is important and mysterious for Kierkegaard in ways that are similar to those in which 'the occasion' is important and mysterious. Now Adorno is critical of 'situation' in Kierkegaard:

> The concept of 'situation', Kierkegaard's own present isolated from historical contingency, corresponds to the concept of 'simultaneity', the revelation that has already occurred. It is true that the concept of 'situation' contains historical, real elements within itself. These laments, however, are isolated and subordinated to the individual. 'Situation', for Kierkegaard, is not—as is objective history for Hegel—graspable through the construction of the concept, but only by the spontaneous decisiveness of the autonomous individual. To put it in the language of idealism, in 'situation' Kierkegaard pursues the indifferentiation of subject and object.[1]

Yet could it not be that the 'indifferentiation of subject and object' that Adorno finds Kierkegaard pursuing is being pursued only because it was already rooted in, or at least implied by, 'situation' itself and in its related expressions, before any Kierkegaardian intervention? Let us take an example. 'In the circumstances' is a short phrase which most of us will use fairly often, but, strictly speaking, is it short enough? Does it not just mean 'in this case'? The circumstances are only circumstances to the extent that they are what a thing is in, yet somehow it is still handy for us to be able to say 'in the circumstances' – especially when the circumstances have been specified. So it is with Kierkegaard's occasion which, he says, 'is nothing in and by itself and is something only in relation to that which it occasions, and in relation to that it is actually nothing' (EOI 238).

Precipitation is, at the best of times, quite hard to understand. We may feel we are witnessing it every time a bird takes wing, or each time we start the car, but what precisely these beginnings are instantiating is hard to name. If event A turned out to be the source of event B on just a single occasion, is this precipitation certain to be characterized as less than wholly necessary? But then if it cannot be so characterized, and if a notion of contingency is thereby overthrown, does not necessity itself – which had acquired meaning only in opposition to a notion now-deposed – also have to take flight? At any rate, the occasion, we are told, 'is always the accidental, and the prodigious paradox is that the accidental is absolutely just as necessary as the necessary' (EOI 234). And just as the possibility that there could be a one-off law of nature (or to put it another way: a precipitation that could never demonstrate obedience to any law or predictability) should perhaps not be ruled out, so in Kierkegaard 'the occasion' is presented as possessing nothing at all *in general* or *as such*:

> Yet it was on the occasion of the occasion of this little review that I wanted to say something rather general about the occasion or about the occasion in general. Very fortunately, it so happens that I have already said what I wanted to say, for the more I deliberate on this matter, the more I am convinced that there is nothing general to be said about it, because there is no occasion in general. If so, then I have come just about as far as I was when I began. The reader must not be angry with me—it is not my fault; it is the occasion's. (EOI 239)

The mystery of how an action starts may not be anything we can solve in this particular work, but in and of itself, it is not a bad place for us to start, if only because the occasion is everywhere in Kierkegaard.

ii. SIN

That Søren Kierkegaard's teaching on sin is broadly orthodox – or perhaps we should rather say, rooted in orthodoxy (he does after all make challenging claims about sin – that it includes despair, for example, as we shall discuss in Chapter 5) – might cause it to be overlooked in a summary of his key concerns. Many of the themes we tend to think of as 'Kierkegaardian' come to be viewed as such because Kierkegaard himself has made alterations or extensions to an existing concept in such a way as to give us what is effectively new terminology. Either that or a concept will be explored dialectically to the point where further mentions of it signify something richer than or different from a traditional usage. Further complexity may arise when we need to attribute a given usage to a particular pseudonym. Sin, however, does not really fall in among the Kierkegaardian concepts whose novel applications have rendered them special, despite its considerable importance in his thought. *Practice in Christianity* (*Indøvelse i Christendom*) tells us:

> Yes, it certainly is cunning if you yourself are not fully aware that you are a sinner. If it is merely a toothache you have, or it is your house that has burned down, but it has escaped you that you are a sinner, then it is cunning. It is cunning of the inviter to say: I heal all sickness, and then when one comes says: I acknowledge only that there is one sickness—sin—of that and from that I heal all of those 'who labour and are burdened', all of those who labour to work themselves out of the power of sin, labour to resist evil, to overcome their weakness, but only manage to be burdened. (PC 61)

There are, nevertheless, penetrating questions being posed for dogmatics by Kierkegaard at many points across the authorship and especially in *The Concept of Anxiety* (also translated as *The Concept of Dread*) by the pseudonymous author Vigilius Haufniensis. Haufniensis wants to take seriously the doctrine of inherited sinfulness but also to retrieve a conception that will not erode the responsibility carried by each and every 'subsequent individual' (we are all the 'subsequent individuals' – coming, as we do, 'after' the fall of man). Now on one hand Haufniensis aspires to uphold an idea that, notwithstanding the fallen state of this world, innocence is lost all over again when a subsequent individual falls into sin. Or – and this begins to get at the heart of the issue – *an* innocence is lost each time it happens. So Haufniensis writes as follows:

> To want to deny that every subsequent individual has and must be assumed to have had a state of innocence analogous to that of Adam would be shocking to everyone and would also annul all thought, because there would then be an individual who is not an individual and who relates himself merely as a specimen [*Exemplar*] to his species, although he would at the same time be regarded as guilty under the category of the individual. (CA 60)

But on the other hand, Haufniensis is worried that the state of innocence will precisely not be analogous because the condition of the world is not that of the Garden of Eden, although Haufniensis takes the trouble to point out that either way there should not be an idea that loss-of-innocence is inevitable in the same way that the continual vanishing of all immediacy is inevitable in Hegel:

> One gets a queer feeling when at this point one finds in works on dogmatics, which otherwise propose to be somewhat orthodox, a reference to Hegel's favoured remark that the nature of the immediate is to be annulled, as though immediacy and innocence were exactly identical [. . .]. (CA 35)

At any rate, Adam is put in a difficult position *vis-à-vis* the subsequent individuals because their starting point will be qualitatively distinct. Haufniensis deliberately chases his tail when he struggles with the thought that if 'sinfulness has come in by something other than sin, the concept would be cancelled', but then again 'if it comes in by sin, then sin is prior to sinfulness' (CA 32). Essentially, the problem then becomes one of the degree to which Adam is viewed as the first man at all:

> The problem is always that of getting Adam included as a member of the race, and precisely in the same sense in which every other individual is included. This is something to which dogmatics should pay attention, especially for the sake of the Atonement. The doctrine that Adam and Christ correspond to each other explains nothing at all but confuses everything. It may be an analogy, but the analogy is conceptually imperfect. Christ alone is an individual who is more than an individual. For this reason he does not come in the beginning but in the fullness of time. (CA 33)

Starting with sinfulness cannot be an option if sinfulness began with a sin. But starting with a sin, the original sin, might mean that Adam has to be classed as a different sort of creature altogether:

> To let the race begin with an individual who stands outside the race is as much a myth of the understanding as is that of letting sinfulness begin in any other way than with sin. What is accomplished is merely to delay the problem, which naturally turns now to man no. 2 for the explanation or, more correctly, to man no. 1, since no. 1 has now become no. 0. (CA 34)

Interestingly enough, it starts to look as if Christianity's contemporary view of the Book of Genesis (although not the contemporary view for those Christians counting themselves 'creationists') – that its truth is fundamentally symbolic, perhaps even more importantly and powerfully true than other parts of the Scriptures precisely for being symbolic, will perform far better and far more instructively under the scrutiny of a Haufniensis than the literal interpretation would be able to do. The modern view gives weight to the process of choosing sin or choosing an alternative to sin and looks at the psychology of that process. It is not that modern Christianity would furnish Haufniensis with answers to all of his queries (and after all, we do not know to what his interest in Genesis remains conceptual), but it is precisely his concept of anxiety that would remain interesting in respect of the priorities of mainstream Christianity today. Meanwhile, the internal contradictions he identifies would be decidedly less catastrophic for schools of thought that have allowed the challenges of Genesis to exist separately from historical accounts of how the universe was made. But it is refreshing, if nothing else, to find in Haufniensis a philosopher who starts with an examination of a doctrine in its own terms. He wrestles with concepts from within what is axiomatic for a doctrine, and this is, after all, the parsimonious method of bringing to light what is problematic in a school. Haufniensis is consistent in his practice, moreover. To take an example:

> Although in the newer science sin has so often been explained as selfishness, it is incomprehensible that it has not been recognised that precisely here lies the difficulty of finding a place for its explanation in any science. For selfishness is precisely the

> particular, and what this signifies only the single individual can know as the single individual, because when it is viewed under universal categories it may signify everything in such a way that it signifies nothing at all. (CA 77)

So he is not really pitting 'the newer science' against the traditional religious narrative; rather he is pointing up a radical problem within this 'newer science', and in a manner that resembles his investigations into the dogmatic issue of hereditary sin. Anybody who has ever wondered about the circularity of that popular summary 'the survival of the fittest' where the sole measure of fitness in question has been – precisely – the fact of survival (so that we are, it turns out, being invited to consider that something has been illuminated by a proposition that survivors are survivors) may also be able to relate to Haufniensis when he says:

> As soon as one wants to speak scientifically about this selfishness, everything is dissolved into tautology [. . .]. Who can forget that natural philosophy found selfishness in all creatures, found it in the movement of the stars that nevertheless are bound in obedience to the laws of the universe, found that the centrifugal force in nature is selfishness. (CA 78)

The *story* of sin, though, was never really going to get more than one book in the authorship devoted to it. And indeed, in some ways it is surprising that there is even this one. *The Concept of Anxiety* probably got written because of Kierkegaard's deep interest in the possible meanings of freedom and, possibly, as a partial result of the apprehensions he may have had about sexuality. The reason why we might consider it surprising that Kierkegaard bothered to invent Vigilius Haufniensis is that the story of how sin came about is not important for any of the three famous spheres. It is not important in the aesthetic sphere, for this is the world in which the question of whether boredom was in fact the root of all evil is much more likely to grab our attention. It is not important for the religious sphere in which sin is not to be focused on as a succession of events but is rather to be understood as *the opposite of faith*. And it is not important in the ethical sphere for reasons that are succinctly summed up, funnily enough, in *The Concept of Anxiety* itself. 'As soon as sin is actually posited', writes Haufniensis, 'ethics is immediately on the spot, and now ethics follows every move sin makes'. But straight away this is followed by: 'How sin came into the world is not the concern of ethics [. . .]' (CA 22) – which, coming so early on in the book, might be considered tantamount to warning readers on a mission to learn how to live better lives to look elsewhere. That impression will be compounded, if such readers should happen to press on regardless, by statements like these:

> But for ethics the possibility of sin never occurs. Ethics never allows itself to be fooled and does not waste time on such deliberations. (CA 23)

This does not mean that *The Concept of Anxiety* is pointless, if only because there is more going on within it than an attempt to chart the history of sin. But perhaps, in the overall context of the authorship, it is rather an anomaly. Moreover, the sort of text that *The Concept of Anxiety* has decided to be, that is to say a kind of treatise, cannot really avoid taking sin – even the sin of the subsequent individual – as a phenomenon, cannot really avoid defining it in the indicative as a fairly distant thing-in-general to which author and reader can refer. However, in the context of self-examination, or of a confession – the occasion of a confession being a context much more close to the heart of Kierkegaard's main preoccupations – there are cautions against consideration of sin *in general*, as we shall now see.

iii. SELF-ACCUSATION

In 'On the Occasion of a Confession' from the *Three Discourses for Imagined Occasions* (not to be confused with the piece in *Upbuilding Discourses in Various Spirits*, appearing under the heading 'Purity of Heart is to Will One Thing' – to which we will be coming later on in this chapter), Kierkegaard tells us that 'the person seeking to understand himself in the consciousness of sin before God does not understand it as a general statement that all people are sinners, because the emphasis is not on this generality' (DIO 29). A great deal was propounded in the twentieth century about how consciousness of one's own death was a fundamental path to authentic individuality, as many of us are only too well aware (those who are not may or may not have all that to look forward to). Further back, however, in the nineteenth century, Kierkegaard was already thinking of the ways that the singularizing effect of the serious contemplation of death may be produced in other ways. 'The person who is making a confession' says Kierkegaard 'is alone – indeed, as alone as a dying person' (DIO 10). Moreover, the wonder and fear to be experienced by one who truly steps back to meditate cannot be acquired in conjunction with another, or communicated directly as part of a team activity.

> But one human being cannot teach another true wonder and true fear. Only when they compress and expand your soul—yours, yes yours, yours alone in the whole world, because you have become alone with the Omnipresent One—only then are they in truth for you. (DIO 25)

In that special solitude, the very fact that no former associate is targeting you, that no denunciation from a neighbour rings out, and that no great accusation thunders down from on high, means that you are at greater liberty to discern the quiet voice of conscience. 'There is no one who accuses except one's thoughts', says Kierkegaard (DIO 10). And while on one hand we are enjoined by the discourse to go right out of our way to meet the one who might require our forgiveness (DIO 12), on the other hand the discourse maintains that 'it is a serious matter if someone forgets to accuse himself before God' (DIO 28). Moreover, the importance of the confession starting with the right thoughts, or, to put it a different way, the importance of the confession *not* starting with the *wrong* thoughts – thoughts about how I am to be justified – is drawn to our attention, along with the observation that in a way we have already started badly, since we have started with sin:

> So now the discourse stands at the beginning. This does not happen through wonder, but truly not through doubt either, because the person who doubts his guilt is only making a bad beginning, or rather he is continuing what was badly begun with sin. (DIO 29)

If starting with a refusal to doubt our guilt (we will return to sin, and the differences between sin as such and particular sins, towards the end of Chapter 4) is not a bad beginning, what sort of things, after that, will Kierkegaard be wanting us to avoid? Whatever we think about unavoidable guilt, are there any sinful actions, ways of living, or ways of thinking that we can avoid in order not to compound that sin we have already? Well, Kierkegaard does not get too involved with particular sins. Rather, we have a set of tropes with him; certain ways of thinking and perceiving – perhaps as potential grounds for particular sins, but also as unloving and thus unholy in and of themselves – are what interest him the most. There is, for example, *comparison*, to which we shall now turn.

iv. COMPARISON

Fundamental to Kierkegaard's understanding of the New Testament is the idea that no form of self-appraisal should feature any comparison of my own ethical performance with that of anybody else. If we consider for a moment how easy it is, in the course of our day-to-day activities, to catch ourselves out doing precisely this, we can see what a tall order is at issue here. In *Without Authority* (*Uden Myndighed*) Kierkegaard writes:

> As soon as anyone comes between you and God, regardless of whether it is someone you consider more nearly perfect than you, or someone you consider less perfect, you acquire a fraudulent criterion, the criterion of human comparison. (WA 129)

Comparison – which the Dane sees as deeply tied up with self-justification – hovers constantly as a temptation to be resisted at all costs. 'All comparison is worldly', says Kierkegaard in 'On the Occasion of a Confession' from *Three Discourses for Imagined Occasions* (*Tre Taler ved tænkte Leiligheder*), 'all emphasis upon it is a worldly attachment in the service of vanity' (DIO 31). And shortly after this he writes: 'when you fast, my listener, anoint your head and wash your face; then for diversion you will not see either that others are more guilty or that others are less guilty' (DIO 31). Here we have a caution against the dangers of comparison *qua* distraction from contemplation of my own guilt, but elsewhere we have strong and colourful warnings about comparison in terms of what Kierkegaard regards as its own special toxicity in respect of my attitude towards others. In the fifth of the first series of deliberations in *Works of Love*, 'Our Duty to Remain in Love's Debt to One Another', we are told:

> Beware of comparison! Comparison is the most disastrous association that love can enter into; comparison is the most dangerous acquaintance love can make; comparison is the worst of all seductions. No seducer is as readily on hand and no seducer is as omnipresent as comparison is as soon as your sidelong glance beckons—yet no seduced person says in his defence, 'Comparison seduced me,' because, indeed, it was he himself who discovered the comparison. (WoL 186)

That sidelong glance is what is so often fatal in Kierkegaard. With love it is crucial that the gaze must never rest upon that which is extrinsic to this action of loving that you yourself have undertaken and that concerns you and only you. It is at the heart of the Pauline doctrine on love (this deliberation is introduced with a quotation from Romans) that love is not to inspect the love of others or even itself. This turning around, or this sidelong glance, pulls a person back into the indicative mood, whereas love whose business is hoping, expecting, waiting in patience, celebrating and seeing – yes – but seeing only what is lovable, has no time for comparison and will struggle unhappily with anything that is like comparison.

> Therefore beware of discovering comparison! Comparison is the noxious shoot that stunts the growth of the tree; the cursed tree becomes a withered shadow, but the noxious shoot flourishes with noxious luxuriance. Comparison is like the neighbour's swampy ground; even if your house is not built upon it, it sinks nevertheless. Comparison is like the secret consumption's hidden worm, which does not die, at least not until it has eaten the life out of love. Comparison is a loathsome rash that turns inward and is eating at the marrow. Therefore beware of comparison in your love! (WoL 186)

We will be returning to love and to *Works of Love* in Chapters 4 and 5, but now let us move on yet again to another arena in which comparison is portrayed as deadly by Kierkegaard. This is the sphere of considering one's position in life and finding it, perhaps, to be unsatisfactory. The first of the three discourses grouped under the heading 'What We Learn from the Lilies in the Field and from the Birds of the Air' is introduced with an extract from the Gospel of Matthew (6:24 to the end) and is entitled 'To Be Contented with Being a Human Being'. 'But alas,' writes Kierkegaard, 'in daily association with people, in the multifarious diversity and its various connections, one forgets through the busy or the worried inventiveness of comparison what it is to be a human being, forgets it because of the diversity among individuals' (UDVS 165). As if in a playful attempt to derive some benefit from such forgetting, Kierkegaard invites us to think ourselves into the positions of lilies and of birds. With the help of personifications that might make us think of La Fontaine or of Aesop, Kierkegaard takes the famous injunctions in Matthew to look at the birds of the air and to look at the lilies in the field and runs with them. He imagines conversations between a lily and a 'naughty bird':

> Instead of putting itself in the lily's place, instead of delighting in its loveliness and delighting in its innocent bliss, the bird would show off in its feeling of freedom by making the lily feel its lack of freedom. Not only that, but the little bird was chatty and talked fast and loose, truthfully and untruthfully, about how in other places there were entirely gorgeous lilies in great abundance, places where there were a rapture and merriment, a fragrance, a brilliance of colours, a singing of birds that were beyond all description. This is how the bird talked, and it usually ended with the comment, humiliating to the lily, that in comparison with that kind of glory the lily looked like nothing—indeed, it was so insignificant that it was a question whether the lily had a right to be called a lily. (UDVS 167)

Notice here the suggestion that what makes the chatter of the bird beguiling is that it proceeds 'truthfully and untruthfully' – it is not a simple matter of talk that could potentially and in all regards be exposed as fabrication in and of itself. What makes comparison insidious, after all, is that it will not necessarily be constructed out of falsity – far from it. If comparison is not always able to conduct its measurements properly, it nevertheless upholds and subscribes to the indicative. Falsehoods can thus be unearthed in principle and if that happens they can be dismissed as contingent – which would perhaps even save the art of comparison from falling into disrepute.

Another facet of comparison that makes it horribly insidious – and here we can see just how finely tuned Kierkegaard's powers of perception are when it comes to human psychology – is that comparison is not obviously greedy or covetous in the way it presents its observations, observations that can hardly be regarded as actual demands, or at least which only edge into becoming demands. Rather, comparison assumes the bearing and intonation of reasonableness, and even of common sense:

> To make matters worse, the lily noted that it was becoming exhausted from its worry but then it talked sensibly to itself, yet not so that it banished its worry from its mind, but talked in such a way that it convinced itself that the worry was proper. 'After all, my wish is not a foolish wish,' it said. 'After all, I am not asking for the impossible, to become what I am not, a bird, for example. My wish is only to become a gorgeous lily, or even the most gorgeous.' (UDVS 168)

This evocation may well strike a chord with people in every walk of life who have, from time to time, become concerned about what they should take to be their station in life. The mood here is not so feverish; the atmosphere here conjured is, on the contrary, that of a mood *settling down* and there is even a suggestion – this is what Kierkegaard would see as perilous – that a firm talking-to-oneself could form part of the sobering-up (or apparent sobering-up) that might follow a fever. Comparison, after all, only wishes to inform and enlighten; it cannot be held responsible for any frenzied hankering that may have ensued. It regrets any misunderstanding, etc., and will endeavour to make its policy clearer in the future. The naughty little bird, says Kierkegaard, 'is the restless mentality of comparison, which roams far and wide, fitfully and capriciously, and gleans the morbid knowledge of diversity; and just as the bird did not put itself in the lily's place, comparison does the same thing by either putting the human being in someone else's place or putting someone else in his place' (UDVS 169). And then, when Kierkegaard goes on to discuss the predicament of the wild dove who is tempted into feeling diminished by conversation with one of the well-housed and securely cared-for farmer's doves, we see the same lamentable rationality at work:

> It noted that it was becoming exhausted from cares, but then it talked reasonably to itself, yet not so reasonably that it expelled worry from its thoughts and put its mind to rest but in such a way

> that it convinced itself that its cares were legitimate. 'After all, I am not asking for something unreasonable,' it said, 'or for something impossible; I am not asking to become like the wealthy farmer but merely like one of the healthy doves.' (UDVS 176)

But Kierkegaard's view is nuanced in an important way. For while he does want to elaborate on the well-known Biblical teaching that we do best to limit ourselves to the cares of each day, and while he is eager to illustrate how the preoccupations that stretch into the longer term have a tendency to proliferate in such a way that they degenerate into self-destructive cravings, he also does make a point of recognizing that not everybody lives, as it were, from an inheritance. He acknowledges, moreover, that those with pressing daily needs to be catered for have not necessarily encountered these needs through any dealings with the diabolical menace of comparison. Kierkegaard chooses his words carefully:

> All *worldly* worry has its basis in a person's unwillingness to be contented with being a human being, in his worried craving for distinction by way of comparison. One does not, however, dare to say directly and summarily that *earthly* and *temporal* worry is an invention of comparison, because in actual straitened circumstances a person does not discover his need for food and clothing by way of comparison; the one who lived in solitude among the lilies of the field would also discover it. (UDVS 171)

That said, there are points in the discourse at which Kierkegaard almost appears to have forgotten his own proviso. Indeed he momentarily appears to be flatly contradicting it when he writes: 'Thus it already becomes apparent that worry about making a living is produced by comparison – here, namely, in the terrible way that the human being is not contented with being a human being but wants to compare himself to God, wants to have security by himself, which no human dares to have, and therefore this security is in fact – worry about making a living' (UDVS 178). However, it gradually becomes apparent that what Kierkegaard is really circling in on is the extent to which the activity that can so often go by the name of *making a living* is actually something quite different. On closer inspection, we may discover that a self-hating and self-devouring obsession with being altogether greater and grander has somehow managed, in the midst of the awful fever, to *include* the idea of making a living in such a way that, posing as a premise, this idea 'justifies' a whole host of other concerns which gnaw away at a person and interfere with his or her sleep pattern.

> But it is apparent also in other ways that worry about making a living is produced by comparison, insofar as the worry about making a living is not the actual pressing need of the day today but is the idea of a future need. The comparison is again produced by a person's unwillingness to be contented with being a human being. (UDVS 178–179)

Again, Kierkegaard has chosen his words carefully. He only says that worry about making a living is produced by comparison *insofar as* that worry is *not* the pressing need of the day and, moreover, that it is the *idea* of a future need, rather than, say, a clear-eyed understanding of, and a practical preparation for, the material requirements of tomorrow. So we can see that Kierkegaard is not scoffing at or looking down on those who labour, nor is he even reproaching them with worldliness. Furthermore, in respect of those who are consumed with cravings, who are unable to be contented with being human beings, Kierkegaard is hardly overflowing with admonition. The discourse does not want to chide or terrify the reader. If anything, its tone is one of sympathy; considerable understanding is extended to the unfortunate souls who have been rattled by brooding thoughts of worldly self-betterment, who are tormented by not being among those already in possession of imagined blessings of one kind or another. Kierkegaard does not want people to be tormented. He urges calm, but not the transient calm of settling down sensibly for a period of time while not quite parting company with the wish to be elevated. For in that scenario, there is always the danger that the dormant spores of discontent will again rise up, propagate and wreck an innocent person's peace of mind.[2] But Kierkegaard urges calm.

v. STILLNESS

In Kierkegaard's authorship there are several concepts which appear in the discourse of very different pseudonyms. We know from Kierkegaard as well as we could know from anyone how a word can mean different things depending upon who speaks it. But with some of the key concepts in Kierkegaard our interpretation of the different senses and possible usages of a word is not made easy by having, on one hand, an intense examination of a concept from one of the more 'serious' pseudonyms, or indeed from one of the non-pseudonymous works, and then, on the other hand, an off-hand or even casual treatment from one of the more playful aesthetic pseudonyms. On the contrary, we often find that a given concept will be analyzed and celebrated by a pseudonymous author or editor with as much careful thought as it might be analyzed by Kierkegaard when he is writing as himself.

A great example would be the idea of *stillness*. We have to look closely at what is said about stillness in order to understand how the religious and aesthetic spheres are different. It is not a simple matter of starting with Kierkegaard by knowing already that stillness (or for that matter, immediacy, reflection or recollection) is basically to be associated with religiousness, with ethics or with the lifestyle of the poet. Very few of Kierkegaard's key concepts mean something in general. We always have to think about who is speaking. We always have to think about the mood they have brought along with them. And we always have to be aware of what may be in a person's heart as they speak. In *Works of Love*, Kierkegaard writes that 'In one person's mouth the same words can be so full of substance, so trustworthy, and in another person's mouth they can be like the vague whispering of leaves' (WoL 11); and then later on in that same book he says that there 'is no word in the language that in itself is upbuilding, and there is no word in the language that cannot be said in an upbuilding way and become upbuilding if love is present' (WoL 213).

The variations in the application of concepts across the authorship mean that we are always at risk of becoming woefully approximate when we make pronouncements about, say, *Kierkegaard's concept of stillness*. Perhaps we can slightly dodge the dangers by confining our remarks to the Kierkegaard*ian* concept of stillness, thereby signalling that we are talking of a concept that is merely to be found, acting on its own, as it were, *in* Kierkegaard, as opposed to a concept in the expounded philosophy *of* Søren Kierkegaard. However, this approach will often feel unsatisfactory, or at least highly provisional. A Kierkegaard enthusiast can still come away from a conversation in which he or she has been invited to introduce the thought of the

Danish philosopher feeling that *nothing but nothing* has been imparted, even if the other party has nodded, smiled reassuringly and appeared content.

Our method, then, should be something like this: we take a group of applications of the idea of stillness from across different participants in the authorship; we start by observing any similarities. This done, we look for what, if anything, distinguishes each usage. If nothing definite is distinguishing the usages, we should maybe not straight away suppose that we have established absolutely what Kierkegaard means by stillness, for the issue of who is speaking remains important. But perhaps we will have a sense that *Kierkegaard's concept of stillness* lies within our grasp.

In the third of Kierkegaard's *Discourses at the Communion on Fridays* (*Taler ved Altergangen om Fredagen*), whose prayer leads into a commentary on John 10:27 ('My sheep hear my voice, and I know them, and they follow me'), the emphasis on the actual place of prayer is important. As the occasion for this prayer is a Friday and not a Sunday,[3] the 'noise of the daily activity of life out there sounds almost audibly within this vaulted space, where this sacred stillness is therefore even all the greater' (CDCLA 270). And then Kierkegaard says that '[t]he stillness that public authority can command civilly is nevertheless not godly stillness, but this stillness, while the world makes noise, is the godly stillness'. We noted earlier, in our discussion of occasions in Kierkegaard, that the unauthorised and independent Dane has a special interest in the sorts of sacred occasion that somehow operate at an angle in respect of the traditional times and days for worship and prayer.

> So it was not your duty to come here today; it was a need within you. It was no external summons that determined you; you yourself must have inwardly made the decision; no one could reproach you if you had not come. It is your own free choice to come; you did not do this because the others were doing it, because the others, after all, on this very day went each to his fields, to his business, to his work—but you came to God's house, to the Lord's table. (CDCLA 270)

Now what is interesting in this Gospel of John discourse is that despite the stress placed on the situation of the place of worship – and elsewhere in this discourse, special notice is taken of the altar and the importance of it being *there* that one takes communion – stillness has already become dialectical. It has become dialectical because with the noise of the world outside it is not only a matter of encountering the stillness that is, as it were, *firmly located* in this, the place of worship. Rather, there is also the matter of the stillness that can be *brought along*. Moreover, it is perhaps precisely with the assistance of this actual meditation on the possibility of stillness, and its invitation to 'find' in the hubbub outside an advantage and a support, by virtue of the contrast, that a real reader stands a chance of reaching the described sacred stillness. Let us now look to another appearance of stillness in Kierkegaard.

William Afham is the pseudonymous author of the 'Recollection' at the start of *Stages on Life's Way*: 'In Vino Veritas'. Afham is in search of stillness in order to be able to practice recollection in the full sense. He wants truly to inhabit the spirit of the banquet whose speeches and gestures he wishes to recount. About the difference between memory and recollection he writes:

> To recollect [*erindre*] is by no means the same as to remember [*huske*]. For example, one can remember very well every single detail of an event without thereby recollecting it. (SLW 10)

Illustrating the important distinction further, this William Afham later hypothesizes that '[b]y continually recounting and repeating his life experiences, the criminal becomes such a memory expert at reeling off his life that the ideality of recollection is driven away' (SLW 14). Now Afham is concerned that in order to recollect and not merely to remember the banquet whose conversations he intends to relate to us he needs an appropriate setting. 'The intellectual exuberance, as it overflowed in the heightened mood of the speakers', he decides, 'is best recollected in peaceful tranquillity' (SLW 15). Note that Afham is remembering his thoughts about how best to position himself in order to recollect; he is here recounting the search for a scene from where he will best be able to recollect another situation. (We can assume, or at least hope, that *this* recalling of *that* search is also being conducted in suitably auspicious surroundings of some kind.) Continuing to recall his careful planning, he goes on in an almost Proustian vein: 'Any attempt to assist recollection directly would only miscarry and punish me with the aftertaste of mimicry' (SLW 15–16). There is the sense, or at least the claim, that were the anticipated mental events to be induced in some way, or were they to be engendered after any kind of prodding, the results would in some way tell of the contrivance, albeit only for the one punished 'with an aftertaste of mimicry'. So Afham proceeds as one preparing a space for some visitation or other might proceed, but with the keen wish not to be summoning anything up, rather just to let there be a clearing in readiness. He says:

> So I have deliberately selected an environment on the basis of contrast. I have sought the solitude of the forest, yet not at a time when the forest itself is fantastic. For example, the stillness of the night would not have been conducive, because it, too, is in the power of the fantastic. I have sought nature's peacefulness during the very time when it is itself most placid. I have, therefore, chosen the afternoon light. (SLW 16)

Now we may wonder for a moment if all that is happening is the avoidance of anything too crassly poetic or wild; we may wonder if what is at issue is Afham's impeccably cultivated taste. But in fairness, he only says that the stillness of the night is 'in the power of the fantastic', not that it would be beneath him to attempt a vivid recollection at a time as obvious or as conventionally dramatic as night-time. Besides, we could interpret his circumspection as amounting to an admission that he *would* be susceptible to becoming *terribly poetic* if he chose the stillness of the night as his arena, and that were he do so it could easily be in a way which would interfere with the authentic recollection he seeks. Moreover, he suggests that in the past the night has worked well, but that he does not want to depend upon it:

> Thus I have frequently visited my sequestered nook. I knew it before, long before; by now I have learned not to need night-time in order to find stillness, for here it is always still, always beautiful, but it seems most beautiful now when the autumn sun is having its mid-afternoon repast and the sky becomes a languorous blue when creation takes a deep breath after the heat [. . .]. (SLW 17)

Afham goes on to describe the loveliness of his nook in a manner that is almost reminiscent of an ode. This may indicate that he is in fact not overly concerned about side-stepping the attractions of romanticism and, more importantly for our present discussion, that he is primarily preoccupied with the stillness that may be bestowed upon him by the world as opposed to the stillness that he could *bring along* – as the Kierkegaardian discourse typically phrases it.

> O friendly spirit, you who inhabit these places, thank you for always protecting my stillness, thank you for those hours spent in recollection's pursuits, thank you for that hiding place I call my own! Then stillness grows as the shadows grow, as silence grows: a conjuring formula! Indeed, what is as intoxicating as stillness! For no matter how quickly the drunkard raises the glass to his lips, his intoxication does not increase as quickly as the intoxication created by stillness, which increases with every second! (SLW 17–18)

But in case it should thus appear that Afham, in contrast to the addressee of that third discourse for the Friday Communion, is not going to be building up his inner stillness by offering himself the challenge of a contrasting environment, we should observe that he has earlier shown some awareness of the value of that approach. Earlier on in the piece, he has mused on the fact that '[a]n erotic situation in which the salient feature was the cosy remoteness of rural life can at times be best recollected and inwardly recollected in a theatre, where the surroundings and the noise evoke the contrast' (SLW 13). But Kierkegaard and his authors are not always so optimistic about the hubbub of multifarious distractions, as we shall now see.

vi. THE MULTIPLICITY

> Draw nigh to God, and he will draw nigh to you. Cleanse your hands ye sinners; and purify your hearts, ye double minded. (James 4:8)

Inspired by verse 8 of the fourth chapter of the Epistle of James, Kierkegaard tries, throughout the authorship and especially in the 'Occasional Discourse' that forms the first part of *Upbuilding Discourses in Various Spirits*, to warn his reader about the unhappiness that is to be associated with the concept of *multiplicity*. A multiplicity of what? Kierkegaard does not *always* tell us. At least, he does not always tell us alongside each and every mention of the word. But sometimes he does tell us. For example, we should beware of the disintegration of the self that is imminent when we attach ourselves to many goals, many pleasures, many curiosities, many trivialities or even to one great aim, if that aim is only a *worldly* aim – for in that case the one thing will turn out, he assures us, to have been a multiplicity. The one thing that truly is *one* thing for Kierkegaard is *the good* – which, by implication, is not *of the world*.

About the above-mentioned disintegration, Kierkegaard certainly has valuable insight in that he recognizes that the very condition of being pulled in many directions and divided across many concerns will often deprive a person of a definite clear vantage point from which to apprehend – precisely – *the multiplicity*:

> One can see multiplicity with a distracted mind, see something of it, see it in passing, see it with half an eye, with a divided mind, see it and yet not see it; in busy activity one can be concerned about many things, begin many things, do many things at one time and do them all halfway—but one cannot *confess* without this unity with oneself. (UDVS 19)

That is all very well, we might retort, but supposing that there was no issue about a vantage point, supposing that lack of clear-headedness and self-possession were regarded as contingencies, suppose we took these observations about distractedness to be a separate issue, can we really not say that it is ever *possible* to will one thing if that thing is 'worldly'? If a 'unity with oneself' is possible for the occasion of confession, is it not also a possibility for the one intent on something not so righteous? Has Kierkegaard not heard of the single-minded pursuit of power? But to this, Kierkegaard replies:

> What else is worldly power but dependence; what slave was as unfree as a tyrant! No, the worldly is not one thing; multifarious as it is, in life it is changed into its opposite, in death into nothing, in eternity into a curse upon the person who has willed this one thing. Only the good is one thing in its essence and the very same in every one of its expressions. (UDVS 29–30)

It is interesting, and perhaps the sign of a kind of theoretical optimism in Kierkegaard, that he does not also recognize *pleasure* or indeed *variety* as being the same in every one of its expressions.

Moreover, it is not as if he wishes to remain ignorant of the potential query:

> Is variation, then, willing one thing that remains the same? On the contrary, it is willing one thing that must never be the same; it means to will the multiplicity, and someone who wills in this way is not only double-minded but is also divided in himself. So he wills one thing and in turn immediately wills the opposite, because the unity of pleasure is a delusion and a deception—what he wills if a variety of pleasures. (UDVS 27)

It seems that for Kierkegaard it is not simply the generality of the concept 'good' which enables it to be 'one thing in its essence and the very same in every one of its expressions'; it is something special and unique to the good. Kierkegaard is careful to spell out that the generality of other concepts does not reflect an essential unity. He spells it out, but whether or not he fully demonstrates it is another matter. It could well be that pleasure is inherently multifarious for Kierkegaard, because one is in the final analysis a passive consumer of pleasure, and since one does not have control over that in relation to which one is passive (even if one has chosen passivity) one cannot determine – either in the sense of ensuring or in the sense of ascertaining – that the source of pleasure will be a unity as opposed to a multiplicity. With willing (if willing can be opposed to experiencing), there is at least a possibility of the content being only one thing, and if the content is not one thing, well then, yes: so it is not – but there was this possibility. So it could be that Kierkegaard's thesis is partly that action *as such* – and after all, he does say that Christianity is 'sheer action' (WoL 99) – and preferably without the tangibility *for the agent* of any results (pleasure could of course be the result of some action) is close to goodness, or can be, in a way which aesthetic experience, or actions with results for an agent, are not. The 'sheer' in 'sheer action' does indeed hint at an action without end – without end for the agent, that is.

A related idea comes into view: that to will when one is not willing one thing is not really to will at all, since only the sheer action of willing the good will protect you from all those large and small concessions to the uncontrollable externality of the world that occur *even when* – and perhaps especially when – your 'will' has met with tangible success. And then you must stop willing – and the stopping of anything in Kierkegaard (love, happiness and so on) is almost invariably an index of its fundamental or 'eternal' unreality; a sign that *it never was*. A world in which evil – including what seems to be the most deliberate evil – is really an absence of will, a mere succession of mindless events, which might strike us as quite an interesting if counter-intuitive idea. It is one that could be considered analogous to or even descended from the ancient doctrine of evil being always ultimately reducible to ignorance. There are further grounds for suspecting that Kierkegaard is entertaining a notion that not to will the one thing that the good always and everywhere is would be not to will at all. Let us take another passage:

> Yet it was a delusion, a dreadful delusion, that he willed only one thing, because pleasure and honour and wealth and power and all that is of the world is only seemingly one thing. It is not one thing and does not remain one thing while everything is changed—and while he is changed; it is not the same amid all changes—on the contrary, it is the continually changed. Thus, even if he named only one thing, be it pleasure or honour or wealth, he would not in truth be willing one thing. Or can he really be said to will one thing when the one thing he wills is in itself not one thing, is in itself multiplicity, a dispersion, a sport of changeableness and prey of corruptibility! (UDVS 26–27)

Now if that last question is to be taken seriously, we have to wonder whether we should rescue it from a kind of circularity. Let us just isolate the segment at issue: 'Or can he really be said to will one thing when the one thing he wills is in itself not one thing [?]' (UDVS 27). Now if this question is not to be dismissed either as purely rhetorical in a rather shallow way or even as somehow inane, we may want to see that its real point of postulated uncertainty – the point of uncertainty which even rhetorical questions will usually contain – is at the word 'will', at the mention of the infinitive 'to will'. It presumably is not at the point of 'wills', that is to say, it is not at the conjugation 'he wills'. For that conjugation implicitly refers to what 'he' *merely supposes himself to be doing*. Otherwise, the logic of the question has collapsed in on itself even before we get to 'is in itself not one thing'.

It is typical of Kierkegaardian compression for an implied commentary on psychological blockages and malfunctions of one kind or another (especially relating to self-deception) in a hypothetical individual to be produced and marshalled purely by changes of perspective on a given word across a single sentence. And so in order to read sympathetically we may not wish to jump straight in with a complaint that we are being browbeaten by a logic that is self-fulfilling in what really amounts to a pseudo-question. However, what we *might* infer from 'can he really be said to will one thing [?]' is that Kierkegaard is really wondering whether or not we can take 'him' (this hypothetical character) at what would presumably be 'his word' about what he is doing when the word in question is 'will'. Or, more to the point, our interpretation might be that Kierkegaard is *enjoining* us not to count *willing* as classifiable among those activities (such as running or baking a cake) whose description can ever be reliably derived from the testimony of a putative agent – even when we can grant, for whatever reason or for the sake of argument, that the testimony itself is sincere (as we might have to do for activities like reflecting on love, expecting rain, or rooting for Liverpool).

Well then, in that case, *what is it to will*? And let us just be clear: that question is not, in this case, primarily concerned with whether or not the concepts of the will are made complicated by the possibility of unconscious instances of willing – instances of willing that are present but unacknowledged (and whether or not these should be admitted at all and so on and so forth). Rather, we are asking what it means to will if those instances of willing 'x' (or of what we thought was a willing of 'x') are summarily discounted as not being true instances of willing 'x' in cases wherever the focus – a sighting of 'x' – turns out to have been a mirage. It is not just willing 'x' that is rendered problematic by what Kierkegaard says; it is the essence of willing as such that is made problematic. If a person wills to sail to the edge of the earth, can we really conclude, if it turns out that there is no such place, that this person never truly willed to sail there? He or she may have been under an illusion about the existence of the earth's edge, but was he or she under an illusion – before making this discovery – about *wanting* to find it?

If Kierkegaard is going to stick to his guns on this, but without actually pulverizing the concept of will as such – also a possibility of course – and thus maintain that his hypothetical agent is, as he would say, *double-minded* rather than misinformed, then he is effectively attributing greater knowledge to the agent than is warranted by the scenario; more knowledge than the edge-of-earth-seeker would have until he or she consulted a shipping manual, say. Or, in the case of one who tries to will any one thing that is not *the good*, Kierkegaard attributes more knowledge than he or she would have before reading a book like *Purity of Heart Is to Will One Thing*. Ah, but then is that not the whole point with Kierkegaard – that so many of his statements do indeed only make sense here and now, in the moment of our being addressed by them? What does it matter to Kierkegaard if his books contain things that do not become true until the book is opened and you read them?

CHAPTER 3

IMMEDIACY

i. THE VARIETIES OF IMMEDIACY IN WORKS FROM THE MID-1840s

There is a special gentleness in the writing that Kierkegaard published in 1844 and 1845. Something musical in the shape of the sentences, and the pace of delivery, will evoke well-ventilated thought patterns and the most refined of mental explorations. The discussions of falling in love and marriage, in particular, have an airy and spacious magic to them. Readers will find that the irony, where it occurs, is never laboured or hectoring. Moments of profound humour will be frequent, lightly done, and even at times suggestive of real joy, as well as being dialectically active in the argumentation, such as it is. The pseudonymous *Stages on Life's Way* (*Stadier paa Livets Vei*), published at the end of April in 1845, and also (issued only one day before it) the signed religious work *Three Discourses on Imagined Occasions* (*Tre Taler ved tænkte Leiligheder*) are cases in point. (The latter has also appeared as *Thoughts on Crucial Situations in Human Life*.) The sorrows of, for example, Quidam's diary, or the seriousness of, say, 'At a Graveside' notwithstanding, Kierkegaard's 1845 output would, if a reader wanted to experience first the brighter side of the melancholy Dane, be no bad place to begin. With this in mind, we will start by having a look at the concept of immediacy as it occurs in *Stages on Life's Way*, before turning our attention to the in-depth analysis of immediacy given, a few years later, by the pseudonymous author Anti-Climacus in *The Sickness unto Death* (*Sygdommen til Døden*).

In case it should be thought that immediacy in Kierkegaard is invariably something to be eschewed or at least transcended, it is worth noting that in the course of 'Reflections on Marriage' several different flavours of immediacy emerge. Moreover, there are points at which we might detect a lament that immediacy is indeed a 'stage' – one that has been missed in the lives of one or two earnest or otherwise temperamentally unfitted youths. And of course, Kierkegaard may well have his own life-story in mind when his 'Married Man' (in 'Reflections on Marriage') refers to 'a young man who actually was pure in regard to the erotic, but a young man who, like a prematurely wise child, has skipped a stage in the development of the soul and has begun his life with reflection' (SLW 120). At any rate, we may well see a link with the story of the little Johannes Climacus, whose highly reflective father would only take him on imaginary, rather than merely actual, walks around the city. Of the young man who has 'skipped a stage' and begun his life with reflection, the Married Man writes:

> He is like that solitary fairy who has lost her swan's wings and now sits there abandoned, vainly, despite all her efforts, trying to fly. He has lost the immediacy that carries a person through life, the immediacy without which falling in love is impossible, the immediacy, continually presupposed, that has continually taken him a little further; he is excluded from the benevolence of immediacy, for which one cannot really manage to give thanks since the benevolence always hides itself. (SLW 121–122)

There are a number of attempts in Kierkegaard – for example, those of Johannes Climacus in *Philosophical Fragments* (*Philosophiske Smuler*) and those in the actual book *Johannes Climacus* – to provide a technical account of the concept of immediacy. What Climacus says about immediacy is interesting and important, because for Climacus, immediacy as an epistemological category cannot deceive or disappoint. (Anglo-American philosophers might think of the incorrigibility of 'raw feels' in Richard Rorty.) Approvingly, Climacus notes that

> [t]he Greek sceptic did not deny the correctness of sensation and of immediate cognition, but, said he, error has an utterly different basis—it comes from the conclusions I draw. If I can only avoid drawing conclusions I shall never be deceived [. . .]. (PF/JC 82)

There is a fascinating consonance here with what we find in *Works of Love* (*Kjerlighedens Gjerninger*), whose 'Love Believes All Things – and Yet Is Never Deceived' is bound up with an idea, so dominant in that book as a whole, that inconclusiveness in respect of the neighbour, that is to say, slowness to judge, is a deferral worthy of Christian love. (We will be returning to this inconclusiveness in Chapter 5.) And then in *Johannes Climacus* itself we have the following analysis:

> *Immediacy* is precisely *indeterminateness*. In immediacy there is no relation, for as soon as there is a relation, immediacy is cancelled. *Immediately, therefore, everything is true*, but this truth is untruth the very next moment, *for in immediacy everything is untrue*. If consciousness can remain in immediacy, then the question of truth is cancelled [. . .]. (PF/JC 167)

Now although it might be difficult to hold Kierkegaard to these precise qualifications of immediacy in each and every mention of the term across the authorship, especially where it seems that that term is being deployed in a morally evaluative way, it might still be that the technical account forms a suggestive backdrop for those broader usages. After all, we can see that even in its more general applications, 'immediacy' for most of the pseudonyms will often appear to connote a quite limited *outlook* on existence as such. We know that in Kierkegaard 'immediacy' will be brought in to characterize the life of one who is *trapped in temporality*, for example, or perhaps even the life of *the age* as a whole. And it could be that when we come into contact with ideas like these, we are, to a degree, being led away from the 'immediacy' when it simply means *that which is not mediated* (say, by consciousness), and back towards the more familiar association of 'immediacy' with that which 'just feels' more or less 'present' at a particular point in time. Immediacy, when associated with the sphere called 'aesthetic' by Kierkegaard and his pseudonyms, clearly has as much to do with *the flatness of now* as it has to do with the purity of any *unmediated* access to, say, a number or a melody. At the same time, we do not want to say that there can be no ties or similarities between the two senses (the strict sense that emerges from his discussions of what consciousness amounts to and the more general and perhaps value-laden sense). Far from it, since it could be that the comforts of number and of melody resemble those comforts enjoyed by one wishing to take refuge in the gratification of an instant.

For the time being though, let us be prepared to find the concept of immediacy in Kierkegaard occurring in depictions of a response to life that is fundamentally geared towards the sensual and the spontaneous. Immediacy is not bound only ever to typify a particular world-view – even if on occasion this is what it seems to do, as well we know from the Papers of A in the first part of *Either/Or* (especially in essays like 'Crop Rotation'). Immediacy might in and of itself just be *a moment* in perceiving, or a simple stage in a cycle of apprehension and comprehension. (Indeed, perhaps the character of 'A' is nothing other than a depiction of one who has got stuck in what should have been understood as just this sort of stage or moment; 'A' is perhaps taking – or mistaking – a mere part of consciousness for the whole of consciousness.) In these connections and associations, however, it is not invariably the case that immediacy will appear as shallow, sinful or empty. It is not that unalloyed or unregulated immediacy is bound to lead through depravity to perdition. For one thing, there are plenty of situations whose immediacy cannot be evaluated and have to be regarded as neutral until what is referred to in Kierkegaard as 'the next moment' arrives.

> Who says that a seducer was a seducer at the very first moment? No, he became that at the second moment. When it is a matter of falling in love, it is utterly impossible to determine whether it is a knight or a seducer who is speaking, for the next moment decides that. (SLW 103)

For another thing, it is recognized in Kierkegaard – albeit with the same sort of reserve that St Paul seems to have wanted to convey when allowing for marriage (see 1 Corinthians 7) – that the immediacy of falling in love can and should be preserved in and through the resolution of marriage.

> The difficulty is this: erotic love or falling in love is altogether immediate; marriage is a resolution; yet falling in love must be taken up into marriage or into the resolution: to will to marry—that is, the most immediate of all immediacies must also be the freest resolution, that which is so inexplicable in its immediacy that it must be attributed to a deity must also come about by virtue of deliberation, and such exhaustive deliberation that from it a resolution results. (SLW 102)

Having stated the difficulty thus, our narrator, the 'Married Man' and somewhat mysterious author of 'Reflections on Marriage', pursues the matter of how spontaneity is transformed in the context of marriage, which is and should be all about conscious resolution, even where, if we may borrow the terms of Kant's second critique for a moment, the duty of devotion coincides with an inclination to be so devoted. It is a discussion which we also find in that other 1845 publication, 'On the Occasion of a Wedding', the middle discourse in the above mentioned *Three Discourses on Imagined Occasions*. Our Married Man asks: 'how can this immediacy (falling in love) find its equivalent in an immediacy reached through reflection?' (SLW 123) This is not put in a spirit of objection – this is not an unhappily married man who speaks – but rather in a spirit of wonder at and fascination with what is presumably for him a given, that marriage does produce this other kind of immediacy. Further on in the piece he writes:

> Here, then, I pause at the crucial point: a resolution must be added to falling in love. But a resolution presupposes reflection, but reflection is immediacy's angel of death. (SLW 157)

What happens next is that Kierkegaard oversees the broadening or the enriching of this concept of immediacy. Despite his puzzlement, the Married Man arrives at the thought that while this 'angel of death' that is reflection 'ordinarily goes about calling for death to the immediate, there is still one immediacy it allows to stand – the immediacy of falling in love, which is a wonder' (SLW 157–158). So now the concept is beginning to develop in quite striking ways. And the idea that emerges, especially in the pages that follow that last assertion, is that there can be a distinction between on one hand, the shallow immediacy whose admiration of the beloved is that of a *connoisseur* and, on the other hand, the richer immediacy of love as interaction, communication, responsiveness. At this point in *Stages* we have already been past the speeches of those who might subscribe to the value, or at least uphold the desirability of that first flavour of immediacy (see William Afham's '"In Vino Veritas" – A Recollection'). So we now know – if we did not know already – a little bit about the emptiness of being a connoisseur. But just as we have encountered characters among the Kierkegaardian aesthetes whose eagerness to enhance their enjoyment of life does not preclude and often precisely calls for reflection, so now (and, as it were, conversely) we have an immediacy in the offing that is no more irresponsible or dissolute for being an immediacy than reflection in the hands of a dandy is – just by virtue of being reflection – ennobling.

Just as it is said, moreover, that the best of humans may ultimately be lifted higher even than the angels, so there is a 'new' immediacy, if the Married Man is to be believed, that exceeds reflection in its power and scope, and above all in its importance for real love:

> What the resolution wants now is first of all to hold fast to love. In this new immediacy, which reaches far beyond any reflection, the lover is rescued from becoming a connoisseur; he himself is bowed down under the imperative of duty and raised again in the optative of resolution. (SLW 163)

There could be other examples of a simple immediacy being taken up and transformed by action into a new immediacy, other sequences of events which would trace out that same transition from the poetic to the ethical. To conjure a very simple case: a person is overcome by witnessing some gratuitous act of kindness, let us say. This person is, as it were, so smitten by the spectacle, that he or she is able to move forward from the immediacy of what is merely seen to repeated imitations of the act. There is a spontaneous encounter, yes, and there is this sense of the thing being wonderful to behold. But the crucial point is this: that making the world a fairer or kinder place does not just remain at the level of an enchanting notion. Rather, the kindness that has been observed has been, in Kierkegaardian language, an occasion, and continues to 'act' upon the perceiver and to engender an ethical imitation.

Of course, with a Kierkegaardian 'occasion' we never really know how the precipitation may have occurred, or to what lucky moment precisely we should attribute the blessing. We might hope that, in general, demonstrations of kindness or basic decency will inspire others rather than, say, make them envious or complacent about the possibility of an inspired imitation. Naturally, it could always be that the person who witnessed that kind act and then went and did likewise had actually 'brought along' the kindness with them, as Kierkegaard would say, along with a willingness to be inspired after the slightest of occasions. In that case, the immediacy of what has been witnessed is not so very important, perhaps. Nevertheless, it is by no means clear that the immediacy was purely aesthetic.

Now if, in the realm of ordinary temporal existence, it is hard to trace the occasions, hard to make deductions about the causation that may lie behind all mere correlations and conjunctions, and correspondingly hard to know how we might launch, say, an epidemic of noble or decent behaviour, then it is even harder in the realm of what Kierkegaard calls 'the eternal' to plot the spread of belief. It is hard to know how an idea of intersection of the eternal and the temporal could be seen to map onto the immediacy of a religious awakening at particular points in history. Let us now look at this in connection with one of the uses of immediacy in *Philosophical Fragments* (*Philosophiske Smuler*).

ii. IMMEDIACY AND THE RELIGIOUS FOLLOWER

The concept of immediacy, as we have acknowledged, will often be associated with Kierkegaard's aesthetic sphere, and he himself will frequently argue or imply that there is a strong connection. But for Johannes Climacus, the pseudonymous author of *Philosophical Fragments*, immediacy occurs *as* the access – and also as the limit to the access – that a religious follower may have to whatever it is that has triggered the awakening of belief.

> There is no follower at second hand. The first and the latest generation are essentially alike, except that the latter generation has the occasion in the report of the contemporary generation, whereas the contemporary generation has the occasion in its immediate contemporaneity and therefore owes no generation anything. But this immediate contemporaneity is merely the occasion, and the strongest expression of this is that the follower, if he understood himself, would have to wish that it would be terminated by the departure of the God from the earth. (PF/JC 105)

Passages like these, then, deal with immediacy in a different way. They deal with the immediacy of witnessing; the status and especially the limitations of immediacy *qua* epistemological category. The theme in this extract, as elsewhere in writings by Johannes Climacus, is the quite restricted knowledge that immediacy is able to afford the follower who happened to be a historical contemporary of the one followed. In the view of Climacus, followers like these are not really at an advantage. Often, when we see, we do not see. Even seeing well may actually increase the degree to which we importantly do not see. Part of the Kierkegaardian playfulness of a text like *Philosophical Fragments* is that the terms 'immediacy' and 'contemporaneity' can be moved around in various ways and still make sense or add up to the same argument; we could say that followers who were contemporary had immediacy while the 'contemporaneity' of other generations was or is a later immediacy, or we could say that the followers who were immediately following at the time, as it were, had contemporaneity while the 'immediacy' open to other generations was or is a later contemporaneity.

The 'occasion' in Kierkegaard is, as we have already seen in the previous chapter, depicted as mysterious. It is called a 'category' and stands for the possibility of a prompting event, though its precise content in any given situation is elusive. It is interesting, then, that the immediacy Climacus discusses with regard to the followers is not presented as the apprehension of some object – which would already be complex enough according to most modern philosophy – but mentioned only with reference to its occasion. Indeed it is hard to be sure that this immediacy, by being (discursively) invoked only in relation to what occasioned it, can be counted as an apprehension at all. It is more like a peculiar relatedness to something that is already only an expression for relatedness itself, or for the attempt to posit relatedness. This is enough to make anyone dizzy. Is Climacus playing hard to get? Or is it that he intends to underline something about the fundamental isolation of consciousness? *Fragments*, after all, is permeated by scepticism; perhaps the uncertainty implied by regular deployment of the word 'occasion' is meant to signal not only the fallibility of perception as such, but also the secret and indefinable grounds for religious belief. At any rate, the slenderness of the possible content for the occasion at issue is argued by Climacus to result in the same level of immediacy whether you were a so-called first-hand witness or whether you become a 'follower at second hand' which is why for him, there really is no follower at second hand, strictly speaking.[1] If we look at the paragraph preceding the above extract we see how this has been elaborated:

> The contemporary's report is the occasion for the one who comes later, just as immediate contemporaneity is the occasion for the contemporary, and if the report is what it ought to be (a believer's report), it will then occasion the same ambiguity of awareness that he himself had, occasioned by immediate contemporaneity. If the report is not of this nature, then *either* it is by a historian and does not really deal with the object of faith (just as a contemporary historian who was not a believer narrates one thing and another) *or* it is by a philosopher and does not deal with the object of faith. (PF/JC 104)

Presumably the 'ambiguity of awareness' applies even if the follower at first hand has witnessed miracles and the like. 'The believer', Climacus then goes on to say, 'passes the report on in such a way that no one can accept it directly and immediately' – and of course this is a fascinating twist because if the hearer becomes a believer, then what he or she then has had is, nevertheless, an occasion and, we may suppose, an immediacy – one that would not be inferior to that of the historical contemporary. Climacus, a 'humorist'[2] and philosopher, need not be saying how much the one who came later has been given; he may just as well be stressing how little even the contemporary follower has to go on. The key point seems to be that belief is something absolutely different from what can be reported (for all the contemporary's report may be 'the occasion for the one who comes later'), or even witnessed at first hand. And that goes some way to explaining why the immediacies in Climacus's account are connected only to occasions and not to any special information, which is to say that they – the immediacies – are scarcely described at all. It is almost as if the spread of belief is being portrayed as a succession of causeless or independently caused transformations that nevertheless mimic the spread of something positive, such as a doctrine, password or fashion statement. Should that seem patently absurd, well, it would hardly bother Climacus who, as a mere detached commentator and humorist, would be only too glad and even a little flattered to be of service to the one who dismisses all the reports but at least has the sincerity to face up to the absurdity – yes the same absurdity that confronts the believer (whose belief, if it happens to be *true* – it can never be justified – is as miraculous as any miracle that could actually be seen).

Interestingly enough, the Climacus account (in which there is no significant transfer of information, only the mysterious occasions) is what an atheist might offer as an essay on what belief would have to be if God (or 'the god' as Climacus prefers in *Fragments*) were to exist and if the belief of the followers in question were *also* to be regarded as *true*. The situation of such an atheist could be contrasted with a scenario in which God *was* indeed alive in the universe and in which there were also a number of people taking themselves for followers, perhaps without suspecting that the *belief they believed they had* was non-existent. On the other hand, we can imagine a predicament in which a person *holds the view* that God may well exist, and even that He appeared in time, found followers near the Sea of Galilee and was later betrayed, but also fears that his or her own belief is empty. This could make the person afraid of God's existence.

A terrible pathos would weigh upon the life of such a person. Perhaps he or she loves the religion and practices it in the hope that one day a door will be ajar, and belief will enter in.[3] But in the immediate, there is only the fear that the wretchedness of sin – in which, let us say, the person most assuredly does believe – is precisely what is keeping the door closed. Whether or not to believe in God is not the only drama. There is also the issue of whether to believe in one's own belief, or whether to avoid trying to fool God into thinking that belief is present when it is not, and stick to loving God and to the repentance of sins rather than believing in Him. We can imagine an aspiring follower lying awake at night thinking: 'If God is there and I tell Him and myself that I believe when in fact I do not . . . *He will know!*' What are we to do if we do not feel that we possess the immediacy of the religious follower? Are we to hope and pray that this immediacy may *unbeknownst to us* may be in us – in us as a kind of *hidden immediacy*? And let it be said that here we are using 'immediacy' – so often associated with the aesthetic sphere – in an entirely Kierkegaardian manner, since for Kierkegaard and, as we have seen, for pseudonyms like Johannes Climacus, 'immediacy' can signify precisely: faith. Sympathy must surely be extended to those of us for whom the only clear immediacy is that of sin and sinfulness, but please note – for this is where the pathos and the terror must lie – that this would not be sin as understood in the Kierkegaardian or indeed fundamentally Christian sense of divergence from the will of God, but rather according to terms that make sense all too clearly *before* there is any other immediacy. Can there be salvation for the *independent* sinner? This is not the one who is wrong *because against*

God we are always in the wrong but rather the one who is stricken by the immediacy of being a sinner with regard to existence, and existence alone. Does Kierkegaard have anything for such a one? Lift him up, all you who are able to start with the immediacy of faith: here is one who has not become contemporary with either the resurrection of the body or the life of the world to come. Here is one who is starting with the immediacy of sin. Pangs may come and go, it is true, but here is one who knows well enough – ask him! – that 'the immediate' does not always mean, alas, *the momentary*.

iii. IMMEDIACY IN *THE SICKNESS UNTO DEATH*

So far, we have looked at immediacy as a stage in the Kierkegaardian scheme of how an individual human being might perceive the world, as a stage in the progress through life that this individual might make, and as the only available vantage point for religious belief. We have done this with special attention being paid to works from 1844 and 1845. Now let us move ahead a few years to 1849, the year in which Kierkegaard published *The Sickness unto Death*, and have a look at what kind of work the concept of immediacy is doing. As we do this, we keep in mind that the pseudonymous author here is different – and is meant to be different – from the character who is supposed to have composed the 'Reflections on Marriage' in *Stages on Life's Way*, and indeed from the Søren Kierkegaard who put his name to 'On the Occasion of a Wedding' in *Three Discourses on Imagined Occasions*. We are about to see how immediacy functions in the hands of Anti-Climacus. This is not intended as an exercise in catching Kierkegaard out by isolating discrepancies in how concepts are used across the texts. But where there are similarities, we should make a mental note, since the similarities may enable us to get closer to what it is Kierkegaard means by immediacy, and not just what his pseudonyms mean. Anti-Climacus writes:

> The self is bound up in immediacy with the other in desiring, craving, enjoying etc., yet passively; in its craving, this self is a dative, like the 'me' of a child. Its dialectic is: the pleasant and the unpleasant; its concepts are: good luck, bad luck, fate. (SuD 51)

We note here that immediacy is not occurring as an initial moment in a sequence of events whose culmination may be a rejoining with the ethical in, say, the commitment of marriage. That is to say, immediacy is not an encounter or set of intoxicating encounters with the wild or breathtaking, to be followed by an opportunity to reach out and transform that initial poetry into something just as good but different, such as marriage, or some similar resolution. No, not at all. For here, what is at issue is immediacy as a whole mode of consciousness. Immediacy is not now a name for the innocent and perhaps quite passive selfishness of, say, falling in love, a moment that in addition to being soon surpassed by something more serious, is able to be reclaimed and restored by that later seriousness. For Anti-Climacus, immediacy encompasses much more, and as a whole mode of consciousness, is arguably a categorically distinct piece of terminology from the concept that we meet in books like *Stages*. Naturally, there is much in the quotation above to correspond to what we have learned from 'Reflections on Marriage'. But essentially, the immediacy that is being outlined here in *The Sickness unto Death* is much more like a universal condition, or at least a universal propensity to succumb to a condition. This is a condition whose antidote – which will be decidedly stoical in character – is far, far rarer and more rarefied as a solution or next step than the resolution of marriage has been in relation to the immediacy of falling in love.

Moreover, it is by no means obvious that the much broader (and less poetic) immediacy that Anti-Climacus depicts is something that can be taken up and built upon in the way that the initial immediacy of falling in love can be taken up and transfigured, according to the Married Man, or in the way that the merely pleasant spectacle of a random act of kindness can be turned into a foundation if only one *holds fast* to it. To be sure, Anti-Climacus is *starting with* the immediacy of the typical civilian, just as 'Reflections on Marriage' *starts with* falling in love. But what may prompt us to wonder if immediacy under Anti-Climacus's highly polemical treatment is becoming categorically different is that with Anti-Climacus, immediacy is practically a disorder, albeit an astonishingly prevalent one. In *Stages*, or in our imaginary scenario of the person who is moved to act more kindly by witnessing the kindness of another, the immediacy can, though morally neutral in and of itself, become a ground or basis for something else. Anti-Climacus, however, is no more likely to subsume immediacy – as he portrays it – into the world-view he promotes than a doctor is likely to regard an illness as itself a valid element in the process of recovery. Indeed, it seems unlikely that immediacy in *The Sickness unto Death* could somehow graduate into the 'new immediacy' we meet in *Stages* given that one of Anti-Climacus's main laments is the precariousness of the supposed fulfilments of immediacy:

> By a 'stroke of fate,' that which to the man of immediacy is his whole life, or, insofar as he has a miniscule of reflection, the portion thereof to which he especially clings, is taken from him; in short, he becomes, as he calls it, unhappy [. . .]. (SuD 51)

Here we see how for Anti-Climacus, the concept of immediacy is now covering most or all of what an individual might consider precious in this world. The fragility of this world-view is then underlined by Anti-Climacus when he says of this 'man of immediacy' that 'his immediacy is dealt such a crushing blow that it cannot reproduce itself' and that the result will be despair (a concept we will explore in Chapter 5). And yet if we consider, say, Job – a character close to Kierkegaard's heart about whom he does write elsewhere, and to whom, indeed, he devotes an edifying discourse (EUD 109–124) – we would say neither that Job had failed to move beyond the simple spontaneous immediacy of falling in love discussed in *Stages*, nor that he was so detached from the events of this world that it was not a tremendous piece of self-discipline for him simply to say, after tearing his robe and shaving his head, 'The Lord gave and the Lord took away; blessed be the name of the Lord'. Kierkegaard says that Job 'did not conceal from himself that everything had been taken away from him; therefore the Lord, who had taken it away, remained in his upright soul' (EUD 118).

Furthermore, it is not as if we can say that Job might *already* have broken with immediacy on the grounds that love for his children transcends mere perception, where perception corresponds to a thing or things, as distinct from human interaction in which (though perceptions may be involved) the anticipations and reactions of lovers and friends in dialogue are never at rest. That sort of consideration could be covered by the 'new immediacy' to which our 'Married Man' refers. This would be the immediacy of *conversing*, albeit with gestures and swapped expressions, an immediacy that would not be appropriately connected with words like 'beauty' and 'beautiful' – it would be a form of immediacy that would be qualitatively distinct from, say, the admiration of a mountain. We may take it that Job was not relating to his daughters and sons as beautiful possessions. Nevertheless, immediacy according to Anti-Climacus, let us not forget, appears to include events as terrible as the loss of a spouse. It is a broader delineation of immediacy that we are finding in *The Sickness unto Death*. Here, immediacy can really only be associated with light-mindedness or short-sightedness if one is prepared at the same time to have those qualities associated with most of what Kierkegaard calls 'externality'. So this is all very different from how 'immediacy' functions in, say, *Johannes Climacus* (or 'De Omnibus Dubitandum Est') where the question 'Cannot the consciousness, then, remain in immediacy?' receives the answer that if it could, there *would* in fact *be* no consciousness (PF/JC 167). (Unless, of course, Anti-Climacus is actually denying consciousness proper to the 'man of immediacy' and finding him to be as cold as any stone, a worse than senseless thing – but to argue for complete consistency with Johannes Climacus on that basis seems tenuous.) We should note, also, that in addition to the use of immediacy as a concept for this whole mindset, we also have immediacy as that which features as a phenomenon 'within' the life of immediacy, as that which, as it were, *the immediate life awaits*, as here:

> If everything, all the externals, were to change suddenly, and if his desire were fulfilled, then there would be life in him again, then spontaneity and immediacy would escalate again, and he would begin to live all over again. This is the only way immediacy knows how to strive [. . .]. (SuD 52)

The characterization of immediacy here, as with the previous extracts, presents it as a doomed and habit-riddled mindset, a cycle of dependency. And once again we can make a link with Kierkegaard's contemplation of Job, or rather with the hypothetical character – imagined by Kierkegaard – who does not cope as well as Job.

> If only he might be granted one brief hour, if only he might recover his former glory for a short time so that he might satiate himself with happiness and thereby gain indifference to the pain. Then he abandoned his soul to a burning restlessness. He would not admit to himself whether the enjoyment he craved was worthy of a man, whether he might not thank God that his soul

> had not been so frantic in the time of joy as it had now become; he refused to be dismayed by the thought that his craving was the occasion for his perdition; he refused to be concerned that the worm of craving that would not die in his soul was more wretched than all his wretchedness. (EUD 117)

So in *The Sickness unto Death* it is not just the matter of an eventuality that will intermittently register as a phenomenon in need of a concept, one which would mainly pertain to the times when we are all happily out and about in the springtime, trying not to worry too much about either the future or the past. For Anti-Climacus, it is rather, as we have said already, a case of a whole mindset or mode of consciousness, at least as he writes in *The Sickness unto Death*. (The other Anti-Climacus work, *Practice in Christianity*, has quite a different voice and is in many ways a different sort of book.) But Anti-Climacus goes further again: 'Immediacy actually has no self,' he writes, 'it does not know itself; thus it cannot recognize itself and therefore generally ends in fantasy' (SuD 53). Now here, Anti-Climacus does bring his notion of immediacy into line with what is hinted at in other parts of the authorship. His remarks might not seem out of place were they transplanted into, for example, the letters that Judge Wilhelm writes to his friend the Aesthete in the second part of *Either/Or* (*Enten–Eller*). It should be said, however, that the Judge evidently feels that there is hope for the Aesthete, or 'A' as he is also known. Absorption in the immediate is something that could be said to come and go in the Papers of A. So much is intermittent or episodic with him, after all. So if the Judge were to remark that immediacy 'actually has no self', perhaps as a way of explaining the aesthete's propensity for fantasizing, it would not necessarily be too damning, precisely because A's relation to the condition is ambiguous, or at any rate, not a commitment.

But if we turn back now to Anti-Climacus and recall how all-encompassing his notion of immediacy appears to be, then in that context, this remark that immediacy 'actually has no self' starts to look very serious indeed. So much so that *even* the quality of the despair that is supposed to be connected to immediacy is envisaged as being deficient (for there is a sense in which despair 'proper' does count as the beginning, or *a* beginning for spirit both here and elsewhere in Kierkegaard). According to Anti-Climacus:

> When immediacy despairs, it does not even have enough self to wish or dream that it had become that which it has not become. The man of immediacy helps himself in another way: he wishes to be someone else. This is easily verified by observing immediate persons; when they are in despair, there is nothing they desire more than to have been someone else or to become someone else. (SuD 53)

This desperate situation may well ring bells with today's readers, although it could be that the exact effects of the so-called celebrity culture have not yet been sufficiently well-documented for us to be sure that the Anti-Climacus distinction between wanting to be something different but *as oneself* and actually wanting *tout court* to be somebody else is detectable, national surveys of the ambitions of schoolchildren notwithstanding. But if we feel that the verification Anti-Climacus mentions is not always going to be possible, then it has nevertheless been suggested a few paragraphs before that the only response immediacy can manage when a blow of some kind falls, is to become paralyzed, and this we can well imagine: 'He despairs and faints, and after that lies perfectly still as if he were dead, a trick like "playing dead"; immediacy resembles certain lower animals that have no weapon or means of defence other than to lie perfectly still and pretend that they are dead' (SuD 52). To be petrified in this way does perhaps evoke the idea of an unreflective and indeed unmediated sensation – the mere registering, as it were, of reality – that had been ascribed to the concept of immediacy a few years before *The Sickness unto Death*, in works like *Philosophical Fragments* or the then-unpublished *Johannes Climacus*. But the relation should perhaps be regarded as no more than an analogy.

Now despair 'proper' (if we can put it like that) seems to offer a way out of this pained and vulnerable immediacy for Anti-Climacus. This is interesting when we consider that a concept of immediacy had once been associated with the nonchalant and carefree world-view of the aesthetes as depicted in *Either/Or* and *Stages on Life's Way* (where it is also associated, problematically, with such notions as 'womanliness'). By 1849 the emphasis has shifted such that immediacy is what might become stricken, traumatized and mute. For on the one hand, despair is the sickness, and we will be saying more about this in Chapter 5, which focuses on despair. But on the other hand it is also the opening of a possibility; the potential start of a new form of self-awareness and ultimately even self-possession. It may seem odd to countenance the possibility of *despair* as an 'advance' upon anything and yet, interestingly enough, this is precisely what Anti-Climacus does:

> The advance over pure immediacy manifests itself at once in the fact that despair is not occasioned by a blow, by something happening, but can be brought on by one's capability for reflection, so that despair, when it is present, is not merely a suffering, a succumbing to the external circumstance, but is to a certain degree self-activity, an act. (SuD 54)

But now we have a difficulty. It would not necessarily count as a difficulty within the confines of Anti-Climacus's writings, to be fair. However, in the broader context of the authorship as a whole, and in respect of the question about what we can take away from the philosophy of Søren Kierkegaard, it is a potential difficulty. That despair could be considered an advance of some kind does appear, as we have said, somewhat peculiar and perhaps a little unexpected, but essentially it is unproblematic. What may, on the other hand, be problematic is the idea that despair could be an 'advance' precisely on the basis that consciousness is being raised by what is more than 'merely a suffering' or more than 'a succumbing to the external circumstance' – because despair as 'brought on by one's capability for reflection' is essentially consciousness being expanded through a *making more of the matter*. Why should that be a problem though? It is a problem in respect of Kierkegaard's urging of us, elsewhere in the authorship, *not* to make more of the matter, but rather to bear burdens lightly if at all possible. Specifically, there is an idea that if we could only allow a suffering to be no more and no less than what it 'is' we would be the better for it. It will be observed that speech, a medium for reflection, is hit upon in what follows as the nub of the matter:

> For the lily, to suffer is to suffer, neither more nor less. Yet when to suffer is neither more nor less than to suffer, the suffering is particularised as much as possible and made as small as possible. The suffering cannot become less, since it indeed *is* and therefore is what it is. But on the other hand, the suffering can become immensely greater when it does not remain exactly what it is, neither more nor less. When the suffering is neither more nor less,

> that is, when it is only the definite suffering that it is, it is, even if it were the greatest suffering, the least that it can be. But when it becomes indefinite how great the suffering actually is, the suffering becomes greater; this indefiniteness increases the suffering immensely. This indefiniteness appears just because of this dubious advantage of the human being, the ability to speak. (WA 16)

What we have here, in a way, is precisely an extolling of the virtues *of* immediacy. We may, in passing, query the suggestion that the limits of what the suffering 'is' could in principle be established with the definiteness whose absence, once there is an alphabet through which sorrows may be told, is here lamented. We may, furthermore, wish to contest the notion – with precisely the petrified immediacies of *The Sickness unto Death* in mind – that suffering without the reflection that would be required to apprehend a possible end to such suffering would in any sense be preferable. (This might be one of the many reasons for regarding, say, the mistreatment of animals as particularly abominable.) But germane to what we are addressing in this chapter is that if we pause and turn to one of Kierkegaard's Matthew-inspired contemplations of the lilies and the birds we suddenly have a fairly compelling recommendation of the very immediacy Anti-Climacus would like us to transcend. And let there be no mistake about it, immediacy is what we are meant to be learning from the lily:

> [The lily] does not ask in advance what kind of a summer it will be this year, how long or how short. No, it is silent and waits—that is how simple it is. But still it is never deceived, something that can only happen to sagacity, not to simplicity, which does not deceive and is not deceived. (WA 14)

Yes, because here we find the characteristic of immediacy that, for example, Johannes Climacus attributes to the conception of the Greek sceptics, *viz.* that there can be no disputing it until *conclusions* are drawn. In respect of 'immediate cognition' says Climacus '[i]f I can only avoid drawing conclusions I shall never be deceived' (PF/JC, 82).

There are, of course, other places in Kierkegaard's authorship in which a decision to avoid conclusions can have the happy consequence that one 'will never be deceived' and one of them is *Works of Love*. We will discuss this book and others in Chapter 4.

CHAPTER 4

ETHICS AND LOVE

i. IN SEARCH OF THE ETHICAL

Where should we begin the search for the ethical in Kierkegaard? University syllabuses may not always have started with the most representative texts, if ethics, at any rate, is to be the subject under consideration. In the introduction to her in-depth analysis of *Works of Love* (*Kjerlighedens Gjerninger*), Kierkegaard expert M. Jamie Ferreira makes the following observation:

> Those interested in discovering what Kierkegaard has to say on ethics or relationships between people most often turn to *Either/Or II* and *Fear and Trembling*. But these books are written by pseudonyms, authors created by Kierkegaard, who present partial perspectives on the ethical. Although in the pseudonymous writings one may discern important anticipations of the ethic found in *Works of Love*, I suggest that they can only be appreciated properly when seen in relation to this work.[1]

Ferreira is quite right to note this and to express reservations about it. While the letters of Judge Wilhelm or 'B' to his young friend in the second part of *Either/Or* (*Enten–Eller*) have passages of great power and perspicacity and while Kierkegaard himself, according to T. H. Croxall, *started with* those letters,[2] it could be argued that the focus on the ethical here takes the form – in ways that have clearly influenced later existentialism – of an analysis and theory of *the self*, as Anthony Rudd has pointed out.[3] Not surprisingly, therefore, much of the commentary on the 'Papers of B' has implicitly treated the ethical as that which needs to start with attention to 'self' rather than with attention to 'other'; it could be said that in *Works of Love*, by contrast, it is the 'other' that has priority. This is not to say that the 'deliberations' of that book do not still centre around a self that *acts*, but there is far less emphasis upon the structure of a self and upon the need for a coherence of self-possession than there is in *Either/Or II*. The connections between *Works of Love* and the philosophy of Emmanuel Levinas, for whom true subjectivity only actually emerges in a response to another are numerous and have now been explored quite extensively.[4]

Moreover, to the extent that Judge Wilhelm's theories about *the self that chooses itself* do have a bearing upon how the ethical could be understood, much of the criticism directed at this particular pseudonym in the existing secondary literature reads more like an evaluation of existentialism as such – to the extent that all those well-known Sartrian claims about autonomy are read in purely indicative mood (as opposed to being themselves *existential*) – and leave out the more mystical element in Kierkegaard's mentions of freedom; freedom as precisely *freedom to embrace the necessary* perhaps with *gratitude*, as with Judge Wilhelm's gladness in respect of some of the daily servitudes that go with civil life or perhaps with *patience*, as with more difficult and more unhappy burdens or curtailments.

So by all means go ahead and read the 'Papers of B' alongside Jean-Paul Sartre if that takes your fancy, but then read them again alongside Kierkegaard's 'Every Good and Every Perfect Gift' discourses (EUD 32–48, 125–158). Reflecting on Judge Wilhelm, Josiah Thompson, for example, writes:

> How can the accidents of a person's birth, the fact that he was born in one century and not another, that his parents were white or black, that his body is ugly or beautiful, his mind quick or slow—how can such facts be 'translated from necessity to freedom'? For the individual does not cause his givenness; it stands outside him, supporting the only freedom he can aspire to—the possibility of determining its meaning. One can vaguely understand what it might be like to achieve such a translation: the resistance of the world, its otherness, would have been banished. But in understanding this, one also understands that such a proposal is only imaginative fancy, the wish of a mind that still desperately wants to escape its worldly condition.[5]

This is all very fair and reasonable, and indeed, failure to take account of the sorts of points being made here *about life in general* could lead a person into the sort of hard-line libertarian thinking that opposes protection of society's most vulnerable by any other means than charity. However, Kierkegaard is no fool. On some level he knows all this and so we should maybe countenance the idea that the Dane is fundamentally changing the meaning of the concept 'freedom'. What is presented here as a poor second to the thicker and stronger freedoms that may have been wished for – 'the possibility of determining [the] meaning [of the individual's givenness]' – is perhaps really at the heart of Kierkegaard's most favoured idea of how 'freedom' is to be used. In *Upbuilding Discourses in Various Spirits* (*Opbyggelige Taler i forskjellig Aand*) Kierkegaard writes:

> Can a person be said to will suffering; is not suffering something he must be forced into against his will? If he can be excused from it, can he then will it; and if he is bound in it, can he then be said to will it? If we are to answer this question, let us above all distinguish between what it is to will in the sense of desire and what it is to will in the noble sense of freedom. (UDVS 117)

And what is this 'noble sense of freedom'? Well, we may have to acknowledge that the *translation* of necessity to freedom which is understandably perplexing for Josiah Thompson is very much a translation in the broadest sense of the term. Let us see what answer Kierkegaard gives as he develops his particular idea of freedom:

> Within the suffering person himself there is a traitorous resistance that is allied with the dreadfulness of unavoidability, and united they would crush him; but patience, despite this, submits to the suffering and in just that way finds itself free in the unavoidable suffering. (UDVS 118–119)

It is interesting that Thompson's concerns and criticisms regarding the freedom or freedoms of Kierkegaard do line up with those made by Theodor W. Adorno – which we will be examining at greater length in Chapter 6. It is especially worthy of note that Thompson concludes – as we shall see Adorno concluding – that a distinction between will and the matter that resists it is being effaced:

> Then too, there is the Judge's supposition that the self can, so to speak, pull itself up by its own bootstraps, banishing despair and becoming actual through one mighty act of will that suddenly, and paradoxically, annihilates the distinction in the self between will and anything else.[6]

It is as if Thompson has not suspected that his own conclusion might be pointing to where Kierkegaard's famous freedom is really to be located. Adorno, as we shall see later, *does* notice where that kind of conclusion (which he shares) points, referring to an 'indifferentiation of subject and object'[7] – but he simply does not think that if we do follow the arrows we will end up anywhere near the ethical, despite all the invitations to perceive Judge Wilhelm as its key advocate. Although again, Adorno is perhaps neglecting the benefits to the ethical that may accrue from the inwardness whose freedom is a form of gratitude or at least an acceptance of the necessary, and for that reason, we should certainly not discard the 'Papers of B' – although they may not be the ideal place in which to start with Kierkegaard's ethical.

By the same token, there is, of course, nothing to stop us looking at and struggling with all the different things that ethics can mean in Kierkegaard's *Fear and Trembling* (*Frygt og Bæven*) – what it might mean when there are mentions of the phrase 'the ethical' and also what it might mean, or how it might be present, aside from any such mentions. We can ask whether the ethics whose 'teleological suspension' is under discussion (taken by some to be essentially Kantian[8] and by others to be essentially Hegelian[9]), is being suspended for the sake of *a different sort of ethics* – one that treats God's will as good by definition – or for the sake of *something other than ethics altogether*. And for those who are set upon starting with *Fear and Trembling*, there is excellent scholarship available.[10]

However, what Abraham has to confront in his ordeal on Mount Moriah appears to be an example of only one of the types of challenge that human agents face when they are trying to find the right way to act. For Abraham, the courses of action between which he must choose do have at least something in common: they are both potential interpretations of the good, though not – pseudonymous author Johannes de Silentio is very clear about this – of the ethical. Of course, what is terrifying is that one of these interpretations is an interpretation based on only one datum – that this has been God's command, and should the datum turn out to have been faulty or misconceived, Abraham, as *Fear and Trembling* puts it, 'is done for'.

But humans do not just struggle to think and act ethically when it is a matter of choosing between competing images of what should be done. We sometimes appear to be struggling to think and act ethically when we have choice between a path to the good on one hand and, on the other hand, *nothing very much at all*. This *nothing-very-much-at-all* may take the form of a plain torpid indifference to acting well in the world, or it may take the form of a wounded resignation in respect of the world. We can fail to give help due to a more or less mindless inertia – even when giving help would cost us little. We can also avoid giving help because we sense that *we* have previously been an injured party and that at *that* time – or in *those* days – there was no help. Failure to give help in this context seems to emerge as a result of seeing the whole world as one single agent, one big agent that has, *after all*, damaged and – *evidently* – contaminated us. When this type of thinking takes hold and does indeed prevent a person from giving help to others, it seems that a kind of narcissism has gained the upper hand; a beneficent world, capable of tending to our needs – *but now perverted* – is the implied premise of a certain sort of wounded indignation. But aside from this, there is a deathliness that hangs over us when we fail to be givers of help. This is especially so if past affliction is what has prevented us; we are putting a stop to the newer self and to the whole new life that can start with an act of kindness.

Now while there might be an *either-or* of sorts here, it will easily be seen that we are not dealing with a *hideous dilemma*. Indeed, we are not dealing with a dilemma at all in the sense that Abraham has a dilemma. The temptations of inertia or of the easy-way style of thinking that justifies a refusal to give assistance to one in need would rarely even strike the one who is overcome by them as amounting to *a rival theory of the good*.

It may be true that when Johannes de Silentio is stepping away from what Ronald M. Green sees as the polemical elements in *Fear and Trembling*, he 'lets us know that what is important in faith is not outer deeds like Abraham's dramatic obedience, but quiet and difficult inner movements of the spirit'. Quite so, but as Green would be ready to acknowledge – and perhaps observe, in view of his own very pertinent misgivings about starting with *Fear and*

Trembling as our guide to an idea on ethics[11] – we are then into a discussion about faith, albeit with references to the ethical, rather than a discussion of ethics.

Fortunately, Kierkegaard does not focus his attention exclusively upon what counts as right action in the context of hideous dilemmas – Abrahamic or otherwise. Nor is he interested only in the point of decision-making at which the self-love of an aesthete is conquered by the appeal of the ethical. To be sure, these topic areas are covered at length in the pseudonymous authorship and accordingly in the literature on Kierkegaard's life and works. However, it should not be overlooked that willing the good on a day-by-day basis is a major theme in the still rather neglected signed works. Some of the key discussions in those texts take place far away from tragic and momentous dilemmas and a fair distance away from (or perhaps a fair time *after*) Kierkegaard's famous qualitative leap; the point of 'conversion' to the values and priorities of another sphere.

Starting with *Fear and Trembling*, captivating though that work may be, in order to gain an understanding of what ethics or even 'the ethical' really means for *Kierkegaard* has disadvantages. At least, it has disadvantages for as long as *our* decision as readers, when we put the question, is that 'ethics' will remain a term that concerns, above all, the responsibilities that individuals have for one another's welfare (which is not to rule out that there could be such a thing as ethical responsibility towards oneself, as is noted by Clare Carlisle[12]). This is not simply because *Fear and Trembling* is the work of a pseudonymous author, though that much certainly should be kept in mind, as we saw Ferreira point out. It is also because the portrayals of what can generally be recognized as ethical existence are either somewhat abstract – as with the characterization of ethics as 'the universal' (FT/R 68) and as requiring external expression (FT/R 69) – or they are connected to the having of natural human affections (filial, maternal and paternal) – affections which, elsewhere in Kierkegaard, appear as contexts or bases for ethical responsibility rather than as the primary substance of what is ethical. Newcomers to Kierkegaard will often choose or be given *Fear and Trembling* to read first, or second or maybe third. And since there can be no doubting the poetic power of this text, this may not be bad thing, for it is, after all, a book that leaves the reader wanting more. But if, when it comes to Kierkegaard's teaching on ethics, the goal is really to get at the stuff of the matter, starting with a text like *Works of Love*, in which Kierkegaard writes, as himself, about the daily substance of our responsibilities to our fellow creatures, might be advisable. M. Jamie Ferreira again:

> Without moving forward to *Works of Love*, scholarship can only unfairly evaluate Kierkegaard's various contributions to ethics; yet some of the most popular accounts of Kierkegaard's place in the history of ethics have been done solely from the limited perspective of the pseudonymous works.[13]

Moreover, if we choose our texts carefully, we may be able, in order to be sure of starting out by giving Kierkegaard the benefit of the doubt, to circumnavigate some of the terminology that in the eyes of some commentators, such as Theodor Adorno, is already contaminated by a philosophy of immanence that has sought in vain to attain real engagement with ethical; terminology which may even be seen as constituting a token or index of that failure. In Chapter 2, for example, we looked at Kierkegaard's concept of *the occasion*. Here is what Adorno says:

> Ethical concretion therefore remains as abstract as the mystical act, as the mere 'choice of choice.' This choosing constitutes the schema of all of Kierkegaard's dialectics. Bound to no ontic content, transforming all being into an 'occasion' for its own activity, Kierkegaard's dialectic exempts itself from material definition. It is immanent and in its immanence infinite.[14]

Associated most readily, perhaps, with the gymnastics of the imagination that we find in his aesthetic sphere, it is interesting that Adorno finds it persisting as a problem beyond that sphere. Adorno gives no sense of having found 'the occasion' transfigured in the discourse of non-aesthetic pseudonyms. So if there is validity in what Adorno says here, we may do well to look for the best of Kierkegaard's ethical in the places where 'the occasion' – as a starting point that might ultimately be pivotal only for the *poetic nature* – is somewhat in abeyance.

ii. STARTING WITH GOD

The teaching of Kierkegaard's *Works of Love* is that we love another person most conscientiously when we love them after starting with a relation to God or 'the neighbour' as a 'middle term'. Specifically, it is proposed that we only understand love as a matter of conscience when we have this all-important 'middle term'. So, for example, in 'Love Is a Matter of Conscience' (First Series, III B) Kierkegaard tells us:

> Before there can be any question of loving conscientiously, love must first be qualified as a matter of conscience. But love is qualified as a matter of conscience only when either God or the neighbour is the middle term, that is, not in erotic love and friendship as such. (WoL 142)

People fall in love and that is certainly a beginning of sorts, but the real love starts with something quite separate from erotic love (*Elskov*). For real love, we must start by having love (*Kjerlighed*) for the other person as a *neighbour*. Kierkegaard describes the need to love the neighbour as a form of wealth, qualifying this by saying that the one who has the need to love the neighbour 'does not need people just to have somebody to love, but he needs to love people' (WoL 67) – and follows this by presenting God as the 'middle term' and by giving that question all of questions 'Who is my neighbour?' a difficult answer:

> Yet there is no pride or haughtiness in this wealth, because God is the middle term, and eternity's *shall* binds and guides this great need so that it does not go astray and turn into pride. But there are no limits to the objects, because the neighbour is all human beings, unconditionally every human being. (WoL 67)

Are we, then, supposed to place the activity of relating to God above or ahead of the love we offer our husbands, wives and close friends? Kierkegaard's response would be that even if such a question were useful or meaningful, those wives and those husbands and those friends will be better served if we start by relating to God. Love is called 'a matter of conscience' and the 'reason for its being a question of conscience is that a human being in his erotic love belongs first and foremost to God' (WoL 143). Even if the friend or the spouse must receive more attention from us than a stranger, it is by virtue of their status as neighbours that we are to be devoted to them. Neighbourliness in respect of the one who happens to be our friend or our spouse will of course have specific content that would be neither appropriate nor helpful in respect of other sorts of neighbour. But we are always to love the neighbour *first* according to Kierkegaard. Indeed the neighbour is even defined as the equivalent of God in certain contexts, as we have seen (WoL 142).

However, Kierkegaard is not demanding that we necessarily start with the welfare of a neighbour *as opposed to* the welfare of a wife or a husband. Rather, we are to start with the welfare of the neighbour, and this neighbour may happen to mean the neighbour that the wife or the husband must always – in the first instance – be to us. That is the key point; that we are to encounter the neighbour that 'unconditionally every human being' is here beside us or in front of us.

> Your wife must first and foremost be to you the neighbour; that she is your wife is then a more precise specification of your particular relationship to each other. But what is the eternal foundation must also be the foundation of every expression of the particular. (WoL 141)

However, we are not to suppose that our immediate *preference* for the company of wife, husband or friends is what counts as loving in us. No, not even if a dimension of neighbourliness *to her* or *to him* or *to the friends* might be, paradoxical though this may seem, the regular assurance that yes, he or she is preferred, or that they, the friends, are preferred (in the ordinary sense of worldly inclination). But the preference that we do in fact feel – that, specifically, is not the love for the neighbour, and Kierkegaard encourages us to avoid confusion in this area.

> No, love the beloved faithfully and tenderly, but let love for the neighbour be the sanctifying element in your union's covenant with God. Love your friend honestly and devotedly, but let love for the neighbour be what you learn from each other in your friendship's confidential relationship with God! (WoL 62)

Now this all seems to fit together quite well. Moreover, it could be coherently maintained that the other person or people retain prior consideration if the covenant with God will protect them from the potential shortcomings and limitations of a love that seeks to operate independently. There might be a kind of healthy pessimism here. But there are points at which Kierkegaard's thoughts with regard to the neighbour can seem qualified by an unearthly detachment that borders on a perspective that is almost inhuman. For example:

> Death cannot deprive you of the neighbour, for if it takes one, life immediately gives you another. Death can deprive you of a friend, because in loving a friend you actually hold together with the friend, but in loving the neighbour you hold together with God; therefore death cannot deprive you of the neighbour. (WoL 65)

However, we should note that Kierkegaard is not expecting the love we have for a friend to be easily replaced. He does not claim that if we constantly commit to remembering the neighbour, we will thereby be spared the pain of losing a friend. He is simply saying that though death may take away the last of your friends, it is unlikely that it will have taken away the last of all your neighbours. There may not be great happiness in this thought. But then Kierkegaard does not claim to be discussing happiness; he is discussing the neighbour. His observations here will only appear unfeeling if it is assumed that by starting with a clause about that living being of which death cannot deprive us, he wants to stack up *reasons to recommend* attachment to the neighbour. But if that initial impression has been given deliberately, then to give Kierkegaard the benefit of the doubt would be to suppose that he is simply leading us from a worldly beginning towards an ethics that has nothing to do with benefit, or advantage, or pleasure in this world.

But what are we to make of the invitation – issued along with repeated references to the importance of a 'middle term' (and with this very special conceptualization of the word 'neighbour') – to relate to God first? For it is frequently in the form of an invitation that the idea of God appears in the writings of Kierkegaard. He tells us, for example, that in the world of the spirit, 'the only one who is shut out is the one who shuts himself out; in the world of the spirit, all are invited' (EUD 335). What are we to make of such invitations? Amidst the horrors of this world, anyone could be forgiven for wanting to decline them, and perhaps even to say 'Let no-one invite me for I do not dance' (PF/JC 8) – along with a firm rejection of that optimistic notion that the only one who is shut out is the one who shuts himself out. Any God that may exist, after all, so often appears to have forgotten about us poor wretched sinners or even to have forsaken the living, suffering creatures of this universe altogether.[15]

Indeed, the humanism promoted by twentieth-century thinkers like Jean-Paul Sartre and Albert Camus[16] prized ethical commitments that would stand wholly apart from the metaphysical and that would in no sense depend upon it. Surely we do not need to relate to a God in order to be loving towards one another, or at least to deal justly with our neighbours; this is how a humanistic atheism could reason. Even humanisms that may be informed and inspired by scripture, such as that of Emmanuel Levinas – whose philosophy supports a certain equivalence of 'neighbour' to 'God' – take it that spirituality must in the first instance be constituted by material commitments to the welfare of others. This is how it is for Levinas, even if our actions in this regard are occasioned by what he would call a 'metaphysical' desire. Divinity in Levinas reaches us via the face of one who is in need of our assistance. God's reality is essentially and most importantly constituted by this claim upon us. It is the calling-out to us – to be understood as a command – of a destitute 'Other'.

Kierkegaardians, however, will fear that we are missing out on something valuable if we straightaway decline that invitation to start by relating to God. If we have found a philosopher like Levinas attractive, we may want to love people first, love them first with all their imperfections; God arises through that very love and in 'the enigma' of the face of our neighbour. Or if, say, we have found the attitudes and inclinations of a Camus or a Sartre compelling, we might want to be defiant in our love and courageous in our ethics, absurdly willing the good against the natural universe. (And here – as with Christianity, funnily enough – rewards for goodness would not come into the matter, or at least would not exceed those of the goodness itself.) It could be argued, moreover, that a special sort of courage is required when one's failures with regard to the ethical are not going to be forgiven *or* punished.

The Christianity in *Works of Love*, though, has a few quite special thoughts to offer to all those wanting to know how best to love an earthly neighbour and also for those wanting never to forget the neighbour that, precisely, is the one they happen most especially to love (in the ordinary sense). Yesterday's existentialists and the atheists of today are welcome and should perhaps not be put off by the primacy of the divine mentioned above. After all, this primacy of the divine in the relation of love for another in *Works of Love* is actually all tied up with the likely limitations, and even the potential poverty of the sort of love that comes from a human being in isolation. And surely if we are sincere about love we would want to do all we can in the face of such likely limitations and potential poverty.

Let us look at the matter this way: it certainly seems to be a fine thing if we announce that loving the neighbour needs no God in heaven or on earth. The announcement of it, moreover, has the tremendous advantage of being ever so quick and easy to do – all the better for pressing ahead and concentrating upon the thing itself: actually loving the neighbour! (It must be acknowledged, furthermore, that the quickness of the announcement will also be very convenient if we just want to press ahead and do something else altogether – but let us grant, for present purposes, that we are firm in our resolve to recall the announcement as merely the beautiful beginning!) Well then, as we have been sensible enough to get the talking done and out of the way, are we now going to go ahead and show one another how the thing itself (that was: *actually loving the neighbour*) is to be done? Can we do this? Let us hope so. But it is also possible that having witnessed what we suppose to be instances of godless good behaviour, instances that show us how it is *possible*, some of us will become complacent in an ensuing supposition that good behaviour is just as *likely* without the thought of God as it is with the thought of God. But in all truth, this *likelihood* is really a new and separate idea and it is indeed merely an ensuing supposition rather than entailed consequence of the *possibility*. That it might be possible for a person to be decent, kind and good without God hardly proves that we would not fare even better in respect of those aims with God or with the thought of God as a 'middle term'.

All power to the one whose attention to loving the neighbour with – *and then without* – the involvement of a thought about God has been exemplary. To be sure, there will be people whose actions for the sake of others are unstinting, though they have no thought at all about starting with God. They might be defiant and psychologically liberated characters that have chosen to be decent, kind and good by virtue – and even in celebratory recognition – of *the absurd*. They might possess the courage or perhaps the emotional agility that is needed to become groundlessly happy in a rejection of nihilism underneath a heaven they nevertheless recognize as empty. We will, of course, meet such godless protagonists as characters in books like *The Plague* (*La peste*), by Albert Camus.[17] And, sure enough, we might also find them – working, perhaps, as nurses, firemen or perhaps just behind a shop counter – in real life. But a Kierkegaardian thinker – even if he or she were actually among the defiant and liberated atheists invoked above – would say that our question should not be about the extent to which the phenomenon of the ethical atheist can be traced, witnessed or documented. Rather, the question should be about how you or I in our own lives right now, this very day, will fare in our attempts to go in peace to love and serve one another. Will we fare just as well when we do not start with Kierkegaard's 'middle term' of God as when we do start in this way? To that we might quite reasonably still say: yes – *yes of course!* And certainly if there can be an ethics or a humanistic love for others that will equip us with as much forbearance (and with as much agnosticism about the character and motivations of others) as the thought of starting with God might do, well, that is all to the good – especially since not everybody has taken up the study or practice of Judaism or Christianity or of any other religion.

However, it is likely that many of us would still feel embarrassed and inadequate if someone were to walk up to us and say: 'Come on then; will you not now show us how this is to be done?' At this point we would perhaps get a sense of the degree to which the humanist ethics we saw as being *perfectly possible in principle* in the absence of God is in fact holding us fast and, on the other hand, the extent to which its hold upon us has lessened. For it is one thing to suppose or to observe that people in general can be ethical as atheists. It is quite another to remember to be ethical in that way ourselves. Do we have the resources immediately to hand? Is our own appraisal of how much we can reasonably be expected to do for the sake of our fellow creatures going to be any clearer and any less open to interpretation than Scripture, or than the thought of starting with God? It may be that Scripture is not always clear. But at the same time, *we* are not always clear to ourselves. Perhaps we are the ones who need someone to show us *how this is to be done*. It is also possible, though, that we would feel embarrassed and inadequate even if we *did* believe in starting with the 'middle term' of God, or starting with the possibility of God, in order then to love the neighbour. But in that case we especially need to be shown examples of *how this is to be done*.

iii. HOW IS IT TO BE DONE?

So who exactly can show us how it is to be done? In Kierkegaard, the figure who is so often showing us how it is to be done is none other than the Apostle Paul. Convinced as Kierkegaard is that we human beings are terribly susceptible to any temptation to defer the moment of waking up to life's most serious requirements, Paul has a certain special appeal. Paul appeals to Kierkegaard for many reasons, but not least because Paul's way of communicating appears to close down the opportunities for procrastination in order, as it were, to put the ball back into our court. Here is what Kierkegaard says in Part III A of *Works of Love*, a 'deliberation' called 'Love Is the Fulfilling of the Law' – based upon Romans 13:10:

> If anyone asks, 'What is love?' Paul answers, 'It is the fulfilling of the law,' and instantly every further question is precluded by that answer. The Law—alas, that is already a prolix matter; but to fulfill the law—well, you yourself perceive that if this is to be achieved there is not a moment to waste. Frequently in this world the whole question 'What is love?' has certainly been asked out of curiosity, and frequently there has been some idler who in answering became involved with the curious asker, and these two, curiosity and idleness liked each other so much that they were almost incapable of becoming tired of each other or of asking and answering the question. (WoL 95)

And here, of course, we see Kierkegaard's characteristic mockery of the detached or 'objective' mentality that has no sense of being addressed, still less accused, by a requirement, but instead wants right away to become a gawping third person – perhaps even a reviewer – in relation to that requirement. So in addition to the many angles from which Kierkegaard sought to criticize and the detached or objective standpoint (what Anthony Rudd calls the 'disengaged view') in the arena of ethical conduct, we now have a sense that, quite apart from any categorical inappropriateness, the standpoint is conducive to procrastination and even, perhaps to complete evasion.

> But Paul does not become involved with the questioner, least of all in prolixities. On the contrary, he imprisons with his answer, imprisons the questioner in obedience under the Law; with his answer he immediately points the direction and gives the impetus to act accordingly. This is not the case only with this answer of Paul's, but it is the case with all of Paul's answers and with all of Christ's answers. (WoL 95)

Kierkegaard has a deep-seated suspicion of *what-is* type questions, the questions that call for a response in the indicative rather than a response in, say, the imperative. A *what-should-I-do* style of questioning, for all it may still precede who knows what evasion or deferment, is at least a decent start. Kierkegaard seems to think that the *what-is* type question of scholarly research, especially when the issue at hand is how we are to live, has often been *a way to avoid starting*:

> How many an individual has not asked, 'What is truth?' and at bottom hoped that it would be a long time before truth would come so close to him that in the same instant it would determine what it was his duty to do at that moment. When the Pharisee, 'in order to justify himself,' asked, 'Who is my neighbour?' he presumably thought that this night develop into a very protracted inquiry, so that it would perhaps take a very long time and then perhaps end with the admission that it was impossible to define the concept 'neighbour' with absolute accuracy—for this very reason he asked the question, to find an escape, to waste time, and to justify himself. (WoL 96–97)

That said, if you give me an instruction, I may genuinely need further information before I can act upon it and in order that I can act effectively. Now of course Kierkegaard would not deny the legitimacy of that request for further details in the context of say, technical instructions. But it could be argued that even in the context of the ethical – and regardless of whether or not this particular Pharisee was trying 'to justify himself' – there *is* a real point to the question 'Who is my neighbour?' Yes, it calls for an indicative statement of some kind; yes, an indicative statement is not (explicitly at least) a further instruction of any kind – *which may indeed be a bit of a relief*; and yes, an indicative statement will certainly help a bit of time to go by since that issuing of the first instruction, which is, of course, all to the good, since time always helps to *put things in perspective a little bit*. Yet at the same time, there is nothing intrinsic to the actual words spoken by the Pharisee that reveals his question to be a bad-faith style of question. And if, after all, in the thick of this complicated life you are trying to help more than one person – let us say two people; perhaps we could even imagine stretching to three people – who exactly *do* you help first? If both parties – or perhaps we could stretch to three – are *the neighbour*, which *neighbour* do I help first? How about the neighbour that appears to be the most neighbourly towards others? It seems reasonable, but wait a minute; what if the neighbour that is not so neighbourly towards others *is more likely to become so* if and when he or she has received our assistance? The first neighbour, our initial favourite, may not *need* the *demonstration* of neighbourly help as much as this other one, though, to be sure, they may still need the help itself.

These considerations only aim to show, however, that there could be questions of the *what-is* or *who-is* variety that may be ethically significant and ethically valuable (just as the study of ethics as such is valuable, even if, *qua* topic area, it operates in the indicative mood and, having distinguished fact and value, must then investigate the fact *of* this or that value). They do not offer up any serious challenge to the Kierkegaardian idea that we can go astray and lose sight of what is essential if we respond to life's demands as if they could be dispatched entirely *in the third person*. So when it comes to whether or not we should train ourselves always to start with the Kierkegaard's 'middle-term', it may not be as important for *me* to lament the impossibility of God on the basis of an evil world – which is not to deny that is evil – as it is to weigh the implications of one sort of orientation for the soul against another.

iv. STARTING WITH MY WRETCHEDNESS

A reasonable self-appraisal for a person not able to embrace the 'middle term' and still less, perhaps, able to call himself or herself a Christian or even religious might be something like this: my wretchedness prevents me. (In the experimental discussion that follows in this and the next subsection, the words 'I', 'me', 'my' and 'mine' are not meant to stand for the author of this book or for any actual person in particular, although naturally they also are not meant to exclude any particular person or persons.) If everything is kept on the plane of the indicative so that the state of the world is held to contradict what God is said to be, then yes, there may be a problem for me, but also, 'I' think, for *everybody*. So the thought of the suffering of the world may be a stumbling block for me, but so could it be for anyone, and moreover, it is *about the world*. However, if the thought is not about what is, but rather about what might be, and then about what *I am to do*, then we have a move into a realm that is less 'in the indicative' and more about what may lie ahead. And in that altered arena, the stumbling block may be different; the question of God's love or otherwise may recede. The questions of whether Christianity is true enough for me and of whether God has been good enough to the world are replaced by the question of whether or not *I* can be good enough to my neighbour for Christianity. Phrases like 'My wretchedness prevents me' or – if one is at least attempting to embrace that 'middle term' – 'My wretchedness obstructs me' would not be wholly pleasing to the Dane; it would be a little bit like the phrase 'One does what one can' about which Kierkegaard's Jutland Priest is concerned in *Either/Or*'s 'Ultimatum':

> The sparrow falls to earth, and in a way it is in the right against God. The lily withers, and in a way it is in the right against God; only man is in the wrong, only for him is it reserved what to everything else was denied, to be in the wrong against God. Should I speak otherwise, should I remind you of a wise saying that you have often heard, one that knows conveniently enough how to explain everything without doing injustice to God or to men? 'Man is a frail being,' it says, 'and it would be absurd of God to ask the impossible of him; one does what one can, and if now and then one is a little negligent, God won't ever forget we are weak and imperfect beings.' Ought I to admire most the lofty conceptions of the divine being this shrewdness betrays, or its deep insight into the human heart, the searching consciousness that ransacks itself and arrives at the comforting and convenient conclusion, 'One does what one can'? (Han. EO 600; EOII 344)

However, it would at least be a step in the right direction for Kierkegaard, if only because the emphasis is on: *my wretchedness*. If we allow Christianity to be posited, if, in deference to what Kierkegaard would call 'the objective' we merely 'grant' Christianity, if we imagine that the suffering of the world could be reversed like a bad dream, or if we suppose, for the sake of argument, that there were actually doctrinal settlements of the contradictions that, on the plane of the indicative, the appearance of suffering in the world engenders for theology – will I *in that case* be a Christian? Or if there is truth in an idea that George Pattison has discussed[18] – that God simply cannot intervene in the necessary, but can only be love, and nothing more – will I *now* be a Christian?[19] Or was there something else?

> Was this, then, your consolation that you said, 'One does what one can'? Was this precisely not the reason for your disquiet, that you did not know within yourself how much it is that a man can do, that at one moment it seemed infinitely much, the next so precious little? (Han. EO 601; EOII 345)

So if there is uncertainty at this point, then perhaps Kierkegaard would want me to wonder if the issue is now quite different: a sense of my own sinfulness, my own wretchedness, my own *being in the wrong*. And if *that* can be envisaged as being the stumbling block that awaits me after what is known by convention as the problem of evil has been bracketed or set aside, then perhaps that is the issue with which I should be starting. If, moreover, the human being were instead to start with an assessment of the extent to which God is in the right, he or she will face the same problem that arises when, according to the Jutland Priest, the faults or virtues of a neighbour or indeed one's own efforts are being evaluated:

> Therefore no more serious doubt, no deeper concern is appeased by the saying, 'One does what one can'. If man is sometimes in the right, sometimes in the wrong, to some extent in the right, to some extent in the wrong, who is it then but man who decides; but then again, in the decision may he not be to some extent in the right, to some extent in the wrong? (Han. EO 601; EOII 346)

If, when we are fully within the indicative mood, we say that belief is beyond us, this may be quite understandable when it is a case of wondering how God can permit disasters. But then if we ask ourselves whether our lives are as permeated with goodness as the life of Jesus, well we may suspect that they are not. If I consider whether I, as a human, have even half the goodness that, as a human, Jesus had in him, well then, I suspect I do not. So *now*, will

I be a Christian? Even if Christianity was just made up by this man, Jesus Christ, or indeed by a man called Paul, it could well be maintained that its thought and teaching – yes, let us just say the thought and teaching attributed to Christ – have more love in them than there is in me, and let us hope that there is some in me. We presume that Kierkegaard would never want to encourage the first part of that thought (although in a sense he might commend it as a willingness to admit that one has been defeated, flattened or 'offended' by the paradox of the God Incarnate). However, it does have one major point in common with the attitude he would encourage, in that the emphasis is upon: *my wretchedness*. Or if there is a God, but a God whose only power is to be love, but who has no hold over the necessity of the world, would not relating to that God stand me in better stead than any free-standing righteousness I can muster on my own? If not, and for some it may be so (but for Kierkegaard, ethics is not about how it is *for some*), very well.

Of course, all this amounts to something rather different from what Kierkegaard and his pseudonyms, Johannes Climacus, Anti-Climacus and Petrus Minor (*The Book on Adler*) claim to be the very crux of Christianity: faith in the paradox – the offence to reason – that was the eternal's appearance in temporality as one who suffered death and was buried and who, on the third day rose again. Nevertheless, we are searching for the ethical here in this chapter. We certainly know the dim view that Kierkegaard took of speculative philosophy's readiness to *accommodate* Christianity by subsuming it as a form of 'picture-thinking'. But how persuasive could Kierkegaard be if he were to repudiate the idea of a religiousness – let us call it 'middle-term religiousness' (something resembling the power of the Holy Spirit perhaps?) – that was brought into being by the will to embrace ethics? Even if he asserted the prior and independent existence of God, could he really say (as he likes to say about so many misuses and misappropriations) that such an approach – that is: starting with the relation to other humans but *as neighbours*, rather than starting with the relation to God – 'makes a fool out of God'? Perhaps he would not be *so* opposed. At any rate, he allows the Jutland Priest occasionally to put the former in front of the latter *on the page*:

> Why did you wish to be in the wrong against a human being? Because you loved! Why did you find it edifying? Because you

> loved! The more you loved, the less time you had to consider whether you were in the right or not; your love had one wish, that you might always be in the wrong. So, too, in your relation to God. (Han. EO 604; EOII 349)

Besides, we are still taking up the Kierkegaardian stance in this key respect: we are putting aside the objective – that is to say, the preoccupation with what may count as *the case*. We are saying that the key question is no longer about whether we judge this world to be the product of a loving God but about how *I* stand in relation to whatever world may be out there and in relation to something that may be able to save me from making this world even worse. Perhaps, though, Kierkegaard would still say that this is 'Good-night Christianity!' But can it really be argued by anybody that it definitely would be a 'Good-night' to Christianity if say we are not sure, and if we do not find ourselves able passionately to subscribe to all the tenets of the faith?

Here we are led to wonder if the criticisms levelled at Kierkegaard by Theodor Haecker, by Brand Blanshard[20] and indeed by his own brother, Peter Christian, have some weight. In different ways and to differing degrees these three all detected in Kierkegaard an intolerance of or at least an impatience with inhibited beginnings, with uncertain progress, with a wavering attitude towards what Kierkegaard himself would be the first to insist *should* be the incomprehensibility of faith. Let us return to our hypothetical case of a person being *tempted* to embrace the 'middle term' but thinking: *my wretchedness prevents me*. And just to reiterate: if we say this, we are already part of the way along what Kierkegaard sees as the right path. That is to say, the problem is understood as *me* and not, for example, *the world*.

Now when I say 'my wretchedness prevents me' do I really mean that my wretchedness prevents me from embracing 'the middle term' that enables me to attend to the neighbour in Kierkegaard's Christian sense, or is it that the wretchedness prevents me from attending to the needs of others as such? Now if it is plainly the latter, then perhaps I am just bad and lazy. But there are two possible ways of understanding the former. One is that my wretchedness prevents me because I cannot or do not accept the faith. The other is that I do accept the faith but my wretchedness prevents me from embracing the 'middle-term' in order to love my neighbour because

I am just weak. But the Jutland Priest has a solution for both of these predicaments as does Kierkegaard's *Works of Love*. We have already touched upon how the solution would work in the first case; if the obstacle to faith is my mixed assessment of what God – if He exists at all – is like then I may be wretched but I am not really and truly *starting with* my wretchedness. Now this solution *is* actually also proffered in relation to the human other in Kierkegaard.

v. TRUE LOVE IS WANTING TO BE IN THE WRONG!

While there can certainly be a double-mindedness in the abasement of finding oneself to be wretched if that discovery becomes the ground for inactivity, it may also be that seeing wretchedness as the best fuel to put in the engine has problems associated. Nevertheless, if the wretchedness has beneath it something else or if the wretchedness is even a product of something else, then according to the Jutland Priest and also according to Kierkegaard, all will be well. And what is that something else? It is love.

> Now if such a person who was the object of your love were to do you a wrong, it would pain you deeply, would it not? You would go over it all carefully, but then you would say, I know within me that I am in the right, this thought will put me at ease. Ah! If you loved him it would not put you at ease, you would look into everything. You would be unable to come to any conclusion than that he was in the wrong, and still that conviction would disquiet you, you would wish that you might be in the wrong, you would try and find something which could count in his defence, and if you did not find it you would find repose only in the thought that you were in the wrong. (Han. EO 602–603; EOII 347–348)

Now initially, the priest has spoken about how it is natural to find yourself in the right when some injustice appears to have been done to you. In a sympathetic way he reflects upon the satisfaction of being able to assure yourself that you are in the right. 'This point of view' – he says – 'is so natural, so comprehensible, so often tested in life, yet it was not through this consideration that we wanted to appease doubt and cure concern, but by considering what was edifying in the thought that we are always in the wrong' (Han. EO 602, EOII 347). And then he asks: 'Can, then, this opposite consideration have the same effect?' Now it must be noted that at this point, Kierkegaard's Priest does turn, in order to discuss the 'opposite consideration' to the relation with one for whom there is some special love already. So we are not necessarily up to love for the neighbour yet, *although* it could be argued (as we have done earlier) that a proper neighbourliness towards one who has the status of beloved or close friend may involve actions that will outwardly resemble those of Kierkegaard's preferential or worldly love. At any rate, it seems clear that the Jutland Priest is laying the ground for the thoughts that will blossom in Kierkegaard's *Works of Love* when he writes:

> You would say, I know I have done right by him. —Ah! No, if you loved him, that thought would only distress you, you would grasp at every probability, and if you found none, you would tear up the account in order to be able to forget it, and you would endeavour to edify yourself with the thought that you were in the wrong. (Han. EO 603; EOII 348)

Yes, and it is certainly true that there is not always that much joy to be had from *being in the right*. Being in the right can be almost like being in prison. Who would not want to be spared all the stiffness and the loneliness of *being in the right*? Who would not want avoid all serious involvement with justified indignation and its attendant responsibilities – or, what might be worse, with the calm self-assurance – of *being in the right*? Does it not feel a bit like having a strange contraption around one's neck in order that one's jaw may be uncomfortably supported? And as for being *proved* right – we can imagine this feeling like an instruction to put on an ill-fitting suit of armour and make a speech. The proof might be welcome, but it could also in some ways be a curtailment of one's liberty. At any rate, the respectability of being right can sometimes really hold a person back in life. Of course, all the facts of the matter can be terribly well-documented – one can work assiduously at it – but really, what *future* is there when one is definitely, unambiguously and thus quite hopelessly *in the right*? But now let us turn our attention to *being in the wrong*. What a relief! When one is in the wrong, there is obviously so much more room for manœuver; a whole new set of opportunities can open up. With being in the wrong, there is, apart from anything else, a way forward, since one can ask to be forgiven. But what scope for that is there if you are unfortunate enough to be in the right?

Now the Kierkegaardian celebration on the love that sees no wrong and his interest in goodness as a kind of perpetual abasement can appear irrational and even as a sign of his position in respect of irrationalism as such. But Kierkegaard is not as irrational as all that. His line on love is all about the edifying thought, it is not that you should necessarily *know* yourself to be in the wrong (notwithstanding his idea that the one who is loving will want to search for evidence against himself or herself); such knowledge, after all, is for him, still a human approximation. If anything, his recurring emphasis on approximations in human knowledge, so far from tumbling into any relativism, subjectivism or irrationalism, rather bespeaks a high ideal – albeit invariably to be disappointed – for truth, and by this, let it be understood, we mean objective truth. It is not that there could be no fact of the matter. Rather, we could argue, it is precisely that Kierkegaard's criteria for establishing objective truth are rigorous. The level of certainty he would require for truth to be objective is higher than the level of certainty that consciousness is likely to be offered by the world. This is not contradicted and is even borne out by the Jutland Priest's remarks about the finite and the infinite, but it is as well to note that behind the stress on edification there lies a kind of joyful pessimism with regard to what the finite could, anyway, ever yield up in terms of a proper verdict.

> So wanting to be in the wrong expresses an infinite relationship, wanting to be in the right, or finding it painful to be in the wrong, expresses a finite relationship! So the edifying, then, is to be always in the wrong for only the infinite edifies, the finite does not! (Han. EO 603; EOII 348)

Naturally, it will be objected that Kierkegaard is effectively shoring up his advocacy of quite radical abasement, if not subjection, with the help of – precisely – the epistemic scruple. We must love without end and without condition because the finite is opaque (or at least penumbral) – *fortunately!* But Kierkegaard really does not have to respond to that objection for any situations where the approximate character of subjectivity's access to the finite can be upheld.

Nevertheless, there is in Kierkegaard a separate problem with this emphasis upon 'always' being in the wrong against God, and he has been criticized on this issue,[21] although it could be one that would confound the efforts of any biblical exegete. About the acceptance of being in the wrong from a religious point of view, the Jutland Priest writes:

> So we endure the pain because we know that it is for our own good, we put trust in managing sometime in the future to put up a stronger resistance, perhaps even coming so far as very seldom really to be in the wrong. This is such a natural point of view, so obvious to everybody. There is, then, something edifying about being in the wrong – that is, inasmuch as by admitting it we improve ourselves with prospects of its occurring more and more rarely. And yet it was not with this consideration that we wanted to appease doubt, but by considering what was edifying in always being in the wrong. (Han. EO 602; EOII 346–347)

So let us draw the chapter to a close by asking about the situation of the one for whom wretchedness is not just a matter of sin in general, but rather a matter of this particular sin and that particular sin, the one for whom the 'always' in 'always in the wrong' is no comfort or consolation, for it is the wrong that dominates his or her thoughts and not the almost pleasant security of the 'always'. And let us also suppose that this person fears that the wrong, the real and true particular wrong has infected them to the degree that they cannot believe or, as Kierkegaard would say 'love freely' – whether it be 'the neighbour' or God on high. What hope is there for such a person? What participation in religiousness could there be?

vi. UNEASY PARTICIPATION

Let us say that I am aware of hopelessly failing to be a Christian at nearly every minute of the day. Let us say that I suspect, as I reach out for Christianity, that *in my case* Christianity could so easily be the indulgence of a completely insane person towards himself or herself. Kierkegaard, especially towards the end of his life had many negative things to say about those who go along to church in an ordinary way (or perhaps, to be fair, they were only ever really directed at *the mentality* of *just* going along to church in an ordinary way). Eventually he was actually imploring his reader to cease all participation in all public worship in order to 'have one and a great guilt less' (M 73–74). But in comparison with the perdition I fear would remain bound up with too hearty an independent embrace of the religion, can we not suppose that *in my case*, ordinary church-going will be less potentially hypocritical or alternatively, less potentially crazy? Can an individual not take the approach of simply letting Christianity be in front of and around him or her, and yes, even the approach of just not daring to deny it, the approach of simply not resisting *its* approach? This certainly does not seem to be very Kierkegaardian. There is nothing terribly ardent or vehement here. Now, any ardour or vehemence on the part of the other church-goers, were it to develop, would possibly be fine and fair enough (and besides we do not want to fall into the dreadful dead-end of *comparison*), but *with me*, let us say, it could either be deranged or it could be an attempt to make a fool, as Kierkegaard would say, out of God.

Now this mere tagging along, this not-being-that-sure, this tendency just to skulk at the back of the place of worship may not pass any test that Kierkegaard would want people to set for themselves. However, it is not a thousand miles away, perhaps not even a hundred miles away, from the condition of the brother who says *no* in the parable (Matthew 21:28–31) of the man who had two sons. Kierkegaard writes approvingly of the one who says 'I will not' to the father who gives the instruction 'Son, go out and work in my vineyard today' – but goes and does the work anyway. This is in contrast to the 'yes-brother' – as Kierkegaard calls him (WoL 93) – who does the exact reverse:

> The yes of the promise is sleep-inducing, but the no, spoken and therefore audible to oneself, is awakening, and repentance is usually not far away. The one who says, 'I will, sir,' is at the same moment pleased with himself; the one who says no becomes almost afraid of himself. (WoL 93).

At any rate, we cannot be sure that the approach of just tagging along with other church-goers, or just going along because it is, after all, free to get in, or because they give you coffee, is definitely or unmistakeably the approach of the one who will eventually deny Christ three times. Poor Peter, after all, had certainly been one of the ardent with his 'Yes, Lord, you know that I love you' (John 21:15) – as Kierkegaard well knew (WoL 155–156). No part of this is meant to suggest that ardent worshippers must be fooling themselves, covering their backs, or running away from the emptiness of which the universe is probably made. Rather, it is simply that if someone who is only starting with the whole business cannot be one of those ardent worshippers (even if they have been *only just* starting with the whole business for quite a while), it is to be hoped that Kierkegaard would not administer a rebuke, since he would certainly not advise anybody to try pulling the wool over God's eyes. The situation is especially dramatic if there is a God. Because, as we have already observed in the last chapter, if I say I believe He is there when I do not really have any immediate sense that He is, *He will know*.

Just as the ardour of others may need to be conceded as quite immediate and perhaps inspired, but not in such a way that there is no room in the practice of a religion for one who is only starting, so, at the same time, the free-standing ethical dispositions of another person, agnostic or atheist as he or she may be, might need to be conceded as being enough for a life that is pleasing to God. After all, that person *may just be a better man or woman than me*. Among those people who are just better at being ethical than me, there will, we ought to suspect, be Christians and atheists. Now I am not good enough to call myself a Christian – well said. But I am also not good enough, let us say, to be a good atheist. In other words, this not-being-good-enough continues as true even if I suspect and sadly lament the prospect that Christianity is not true. It is not as if the former can be liquidated along with the latter. So I am not good enough to call myself a Christian. Am I then good enough to be an atheist with free-standing righteousness? Surely not! If I am not good enough to be a Christian – *when Christ is there to help me* – then most assuredly I am not good enough to be a good atheist! The goal was to establish the concept of the neighbour as a middle-term. If, from the point of view of ethics, there is greater chance of success *in my case* with an alternative to ethical atheism, then even if I cannot seem to get started with Christianity, I may have to pursue what is Christian.

CHAPTER 5

DESPAIR AND HOPE

i. DESPAIR IN *THE SICKNESS UNTO DEATH*

Our strongest impression of what Kierkegaard's concept of despair signifies and entails is almost bound to come from Anti-Climacus's 'Christian Psychological Exposition for Upbuilding and Awakening' – *The Sickness unto Death* (*Sygdommen til Døden*). Anti-Climacus, we will remember, is also the pseudonym for the author of *Practice in Christianity* (*Indøvelse i Christendom*), a book that Kierkegaard nearly issued as a signed work. He stepped back from this idea, however, feeling that he could not personally lay claim to the strength of Christianity embodied in the teaching of that work. It is thus attributed to a character that Kierkegaard felt was higher than himself in terms of closeness to God and in terms of understanding Christianity's requirement (where 'understanding' actually involves living up to the requirement).

In Chapter 3 of this book we saw that the concept of immediacy when addressed by Anti-Climacus is far-reaching in what it covers; dauntingly so, in fact. What for other 'lower' pseudonyms might pass for earnestness could, it seems, be classified as immediacy for Anti-Climacus. The concept of despair in *The Sickness unto Death* is, as it were, correspondingly broad and all-encompassing. There can be no clearer indication of this than the point in the section entitled 'The Universality of this Sickness (Despair)' at which Anti-Climacus tells us that what 'the common view' completely overlooks is 'that not being in despair, not being conscious of being in despair, is precisely a form of despair' (SuD 23). And although Anti-Climacus does, as we can see, call despair 'a sickness of the spirit' (SuD xi), he also says that '[n]ot being in despair is not similar to not being sick, for not being sick cannot be the same as being sick, whereas not being in despair can be the very same as being in despair' (SuD 24–25). This is likely to strike us as problematic; if nobody but nobody is left out of the category of despair, the category will surely become extremely hard to define. Or at least it will become hard to define in any way that does not simply equate it with the human condition as such. When that happens, it is as if what we are dealing with is purely an *assignation* of the concept of despair, rather than an analysis.

Be that as it may, we can still describe the salient features of the various *forms* of despair into which subjectivity can fall, according to Anti-Climacus, or into which it can gradually become ensnared. They are given as follows: *in despair not to be conscious of having a self* – although we are told that this is 'not despair in the strict sense' (SuD ix), *in despair not to will to be oneself* and finally, *in despair to will to be oneself*. Each of these three forms has a dedicated section in 'Part C' of *The Sickness unto Death*. However, this 'Part C' initially has, after a brief introduction, an 'A' section and a 'B' section, with 'B' comprising an 'a' and a 'b' division. And it is only within the 'b' section that the second and third categories of despair (of those listed above) – which are themselves allocated further subdivisions – get defined, the 'a' division having been devoted to 'The Despair That Is Ignorant of Being Despair [. . .].'

Two kinds of suicide are discussed in the 'a' division of the 'B' section of Part C. On one hand we have the pagan view of suicide which, according to Anti-Climacus, lacks a conception of self in that there is no real sense of suicide as *self-murder*.

> [I]n purely pagan thinking, suicide is neutral, something entirely up to the pleasure of each individual since it is no one else's business. If an admonition against suicide were to be given from the viewpoint of paganism, it would have to be in the long, roundabout way of showing that suicide violates the relation of obligation to others. (SuD 46)

In Christianity, by contrast, suicide is, according to Anti-Climacus, 'a crime against God' (SuD 46). Correspondingly, and insomuch as the devout Christian could or would be aware of the prohibition against self-slaughter, Anti-Climacus maintains that there is an especially intense despair in the one who commits suicide in spite of an awareness that suicide is despair (that is to say, suicide is judged symptomatic in addition to being reactive) and, perhaps, that despair is sin – which Anti-Climacus also argues. So for example, we have:

> The person who, with a realization that suicide is despair and to that extent with a true conception of the nature of despair, commits suicide is more intensively in despair than one who commits suicide without a clear idea that suicide is despair; conversely, the less true his conception, the less intensive his despair. (SuD 47)

Now of course, if these teachings on suicide are taken to heart by the individual with Christian aspirations who sees nevertheless that the horrors and miseries of his or her life are altogether intractable, the situation is grave. It may be less grave for the Christian, or aspiring Christian who has a faith, or who has a degree of faith, even if we grant that for this other type of individual the horrors and miseries remain intractable. This is because faith holds out the hope of salvation and thus the temptation of suicide can be resisted rationally – rationally that is, after faith has been found or granted (in life) or postulated (here). But for the one who seeks to live according to God's laws inside a life that is unbearable, yet with no sense that salvation can come without there having been faith, the situation is grave. Beyond the obligation to others mentioned above (let us suppose it is a case where there are no others to be significantly affected), any refusal of suicide will be rational only in respect of a plain fear (one that would not presuppose faith in the Kierkegaardian sense) that punishment awaits the one whose final act has been a sin – a 'crime against God', no less – rather than an act of repentance. At the same time, there is no hope that enduring the miseries will pave the way to redemption, be it in the shape of a life everlasting or, more importantly, through the forgiveness of sins. Such a one, it seems, will be damned either way, like a person who lies down but finds no comfort doing that, and so stands, but finds no comfort doing that (Han. EO 43; EOI 20).

However, all these considerations are considerations arising from a dogma alluded to, not quite parenthetically but as a kind of subordinate clause, in the meditation upon despair that we find in the second half of 'Part C'. For the whole issue of suicide, it could be argued, is only introduced by Anti-Climacus at this point in order to illustrate a contrast in the conceptions of self that we will find in paganism on one hand, and in Christianity on the other. And of course it is with the question of what counts as a self that *The Sickness unto Death* begins.

The self, Kierkegaard fears, is what will easily be overlooked when the natural man has been stricken or convulsed by a loss. We think of Kierkegaard as a philosopher who goes deeply into despair, and indeed he does. But wherever despair appears in Kierkegaard, there will straight away be a question about whether a self is going to be affected. Is despair going to be the occasion for selfhood's disintegration? Is despair going to cause the sufferer to forget that he or she may still have a self, or to abandon the effort to become a self? Or is despair going to be the occasion for noticing that one is or could be a self? Now these questions can be subdivided in accordance with how despair is being understood in any given context.

If by 'despair' we mean the sorrow and pain following the terrible events that can befall a person, then the question might be about whether we can be courageous enough to remember the reality of what it is that has been lost, a form of remembrance that for religiousness will take the form of thankfulness. In this case it is to the figure of Job that Kierkegaard will turn. Kierkegaard admires Job for holding together in his mind the reality of what he has loved and the reality of its disappearance. Students of Kierkegaard are often encouraged to start by looking at his Abraham, or rather, at his various Abrahams. But, properly understood and taken seriously, *Fear and Trembling* (*Frygt og Bæven*) could be a very hard place to start. Contemplation of Job's ordeal is also quite difficult, but in a different way. Starting with Job is an option that should not be ruled out. And sure enough, Job does come along quite early in the authorship, in the December of 1843, to be precise. The first of that month's 'Four Upbuilding Discourses' entitled 'The Lord gave and the Lord took away; blessed be the Name of the Lord' contains recognition of the devastating effects of personal loss. But, as if to prepare us for the possibility that the most serious and eminently justifiable grief could stray from itself by turning into something more egocentric, Kierkegaard also considers the common, if not natural reaction to the disappearance of any external grounds for happiness. Let us look again at the extract quoted in Chapter 3:

> If only he might be granted one brief hour, if only he might recover his former glory for a short time so that he might satiate

> himself with happiness and thereby gain indifference to the pain. Then he abandoned his soul to a burning restlessness. He would not admit to himself whether the enjoyment he craved was worthy of a man, whether he might not thank God that his soul had not been so frantic in the time of joy as it had now become; he refused to be dismayed by the thought that his craving was the occasion for his perdition; he refused to be concerned that the worm of craving that would not die in his soul was more wretched than all his wretchedness. (EUD 117)

See here how the occasion for the wretchedness mentioned is acknowledged to be 'the pain' – we are not dealing here with a wretchedness that could not in worldly terms be understood or even justified. Indeed, the circumstances perhaps *should* be found mitigating in worldly terms were the soul described above ever to exist as a real person being referred to in the third person. Discourses by Kierkegaard, however, are *unworldly* in addressing 'you' and even their invocations of hypothetical third persons are to be construed as part of that address. The wretchedness, nevertheless, is acknowledged to have been occasioned and does not, in this case, emerge *ex nihilo*, as it were. So it may not have the flavour of, say, the anxiety over nothingness which Vigilius Haufniensis thinks of as preceding sin. The wretchedness has been occasioned, perhaps horribly and arbitrarily occasioned, and results in something resembling Simone Weil's notion of *affliction*.

Why then, is Kierkegaard so stern? Why does he say that '[i]nstead of trying to bear the loss,' the afflicted person 'chose to waste his energies in impotent defiance, in losing himself in a demented possession of what had been lost' (EUD 118) – as if, in addition to being stricken, the person must now be held to account? Yet this is something we find so often in Kierkegaard, that he is not as interested in targeting the one whose wretchedness is gratuitous and without excuse as he is in considering those whose misfortunes might make wretchedness *understandable in the circumstances*. Perhaps it is because the rescue of such people has to be attempted with so much more subtlety. It is a case of getting inside the psychology of affliction and yet at the same time preserving the tone of admonition that might more predictably be associated with an address to the sinner pure and simple: 'Or he mendaciously tried to defraud the good once bestowed on him – as if it had never been splendid, had never made him happy; he thought he could strengthen his soul by wretched self-deceit, as if there were strength in falsehood' (EUD 118). So says Kierkegaard, but not really as an allegation, since, as we have suggested, the hypothetical 'he' is conjured for the sake of *upbuilding*. For all we know, he could be admonishing himself.

Now if, on the other hand, we are interpreting despair in the context of a predicament that is *not* what contemporary expression would call reactive, even if its ultimate source might have been readable in that way, then in a way we are back to *The Sickness unto Death*. But *The Sickness unto Death* is far from being the only essay in which despair is actually established as a snare even for those who do not regard themselves as unfortunate. One of the deliberations in *Works of Love* (*Kjerlighedens Gjerninger*), 'Love Hopes All Things – and Yet Is Never Put to Shame', points to a similar perspective. Here, for example, Kierkegaard tells us that 'anyone who refuses to understand that the whole of one's life should be the time of hope is veritably in despair, no matter, absolutely no matter, whether he is conscious of it or not' (WoL 252) and this 'whether he is conscious of it or not' may well remind us of *The Sickness unto Death*. Indeed, when we line up these texts we will see that they share a good number of preoccupations and other attributes. *Works of Love* was written first, of course, but 'Love Hopes All things' could most be read as the 'happy ending' of the later book, and it is interesting that reference is made to a 'sickness [being] unto death' in this earlier piece from 1847 (WoL 259). The voice of Kierkegaard is distinct from that of Anti-Climacus (and this is not just due to the supposedly sterner requirements of the latter but of the experimentation – albeit playful – with quasi-Hegelian analysis), but there are rich similarities and we should look at some of these.

The consonance is partly a question of the favoured motifs and conceits. Just as possibility in *The Sickness unto Death* is associated with deep breathing, so in 'Love Hopes All Things' we are told that '[w]hen the God-forsaken worldliness of earthly life shuts itself in with itself in complacency, the confined air develops poison in itself and by itself' (WoL 246). And as if to prevent us from becoming disheartened too quickly by this terribly evocative image, Kierkegaard follows it, just a few lines later, by saying:

> See, this is why so often at various times a need is felt for a refreshing, enlivening breeze, a mighty gale, that could cleanse the air and dispel the poisonous vapours, a need for the rescuing

> movement of a great event that rescues by moving what is standing still, a need for the enlivening prospect of a great expectancy – lest we suffocate in worldliness or perish in the oppressing moment! (WoL 246)

But the connections do not end there. For it is in 'Love Hopes All Things' that we find an exploration of one of Kierkegaard's more difficult ideas: the idea of subjectivity – at least when it embraces hopefulness – as constituted by kind of dual-awareness, a dual-awareness, that is, of the temporal and the eternal: 'to hope is composed of the eternal and the temporal, and this is why the expression for hope's task in the form of eternity is to hope all things, and in the form of temporality to hope always' (WoL 249). This may seem tricky, but if anybody has ever been flummoxed or bewildered by Anti-Climacus's discussion of the self as 'a synthesis' in *The Sickness unto Death* of necessity and possibility, they could do worse than start with what Kierkegaard has said here a couple of years before. Psychologically, the eternal is connected with a concept of possibility in 'Love Hopes All Things' and, interestingly enough, given that *The Sickness Unto Death* is meant to be a 'psychological exposition', it is arguably more clear in 'Love Hopes All Things' that we are in the realm of psychology, or that Kierkegaard is undertaking the sort of work that might, had it come after Husserl, have been classified as a phenomenology.

Granted, the *Works of Love* discussion is framed by the sorts of bold announcements that will appear later in *The Sickness unto Death* (whose constative mood seems to have been selected in pointed contrast to that tone of tentative questioning which characterizes the 'Interlude' in *Philosophical Fragments*): '[t]he past is actual, the future is the possible; eternally the eternal is the eternal; in time, the eternal is the possible, the future' (WoL 249). But even here, we are getting some helpful hints that the focus is not ontological, especially with the first part of the sentence being elaborated upon by this remark that *eternally the eternal is the eternal; in time, the eternal is the possible, the future*. But then, as the argument unfolds, things really do start to become clearer:

> Anyone who gives up the possibility that his existence could be forfeited in the next moment—provided he does not give up this possibility because he *hopes* for the possibility of the good—

> anyone who lives without possibility is in despair. He breaks with the eternal and arbitrarily puts an end to possibility; without the consent of eternity, he ends where the end is not [. . .].' (WoL 252)

So here, then, we have a suggestion that actuality – not 'actuality' in the sense of the immediacy craved by a listless aesthete who, with the help of piquant adventures on the streets of Copenhagen, wishes to become *a vigorous champion of actuality*, but in the sense of *what really is going to have been the truth of the whole universe* – could exist, and exist as definitive. Yes, but this actuality exists only as the preserve of what Kierkegaard calls *the eternal* – that which lies outside the comprehension of a human. And temporality's reaching out towards this eternal, or – more to the point – its potentially passionate bid to shape what will, to be sure, become definitive – an eternity, no less – takes these forms in the mind of the agent: *possibility* and *the future*. Here we have it:

> If eternity were to assign the human being the task all at once and in its own language, without regard for his capacities and limited powers, the human being would have to despair. But then this is the wondrous thing, that this greatest of powers, eternity, can make itself so small that it is divisible in this way, this which is eternally one, so that taking upon itself the form of the future, the possible, with the help of hope it beings up temporality's child (the human being), teaches him to hope (to hope is itself the instruction, is the relation to the eternal), provided he does not arbitrarily choose to be severely disheartened by fear or brazenly choose to despair—that is, to withdraw from the upbringing by possibility. (WoL 252–253)

Fatalism in respect of any particular outcome or outcomes cannot be deduced from the recognition that all events are interdependent. For one thing, a true recognition of that sort would understand interdependency as vanishing instantly along with the very events which whose individuation it had exposed as arbitrary. (Fatalism that was not in respect of mentionable outcomes would already have turned into something altogether different, such as stoicism.) Determinism can probably be counted defensible on many grounds, but wherever history's chains of precipitation are invoked, there is trouble ahead, since these very chains imply spaces between the items of which they are composed; as if the events were mysteriously suspended in a kind of fluid that was itself somehow less than wholly necessary. Furthermore, and this is where we see yet another prefiguring of *The Sickness unto Death* in the extracts from 'Love Hopes All Things' quoted above, fatalism has *no vantage point* from which to decipher an ending. The eternal, which we assume contains the information to which fatalism would like to gain access, withholds the information and has not, in Kierkegaardian terms, *given consent* for any imposition of an ending.

Science may be quite right when and where it denies the residing in external things of possibility, and it may well be either short-sighted or categorically confounded, when, *out there*, it discovers what it takes to be some sort of inherent possibility. But for the subject then to surrender all hope would be wrong-headed – an artificial (and really insupportable) raising of itself out of the continuum of temporality in which it is – precisely – inextricably embedded. (Determinism, which fatalistic attitudes will typically distort, would quickly and honourably admit as much.) The above extract really does tie in with the idea, so familiar to Kierkegaard's readers, of truth being what is true *for you* (*for dig*).

An easily misunderstood idea of Kierkegaard's, this notion of truth as subjectivity, stated at the very end of *Either/Or* and explored at greater length in the *Postscript*, could be interpreted as meaning that out of all the things that would count as true according to the classical model, or correspondence theory, say, the only things that are true in any important way are those we have appropriated as edifying for us (and these may include things that are already the case as well as states of affairs that come into existence – genuinely – because we have started with an indicative that is really a subjunctive and *presupposed* them). Now while Kierkegaard could conceivably be brought in for questioning over the possible *circularity* of an idea that *only the truth which edifies is true for you* (Han. EO 609; EOII 354) – if it is translated as *only the truth that directly concerns you is what directly concerns you* – he cannot be had up for subjectivism. For indeed, his famous precept leaves objective truth exactly where it is. We could read Kierkegaard as meaning that we are not to spend our time on (or flatter ourselves with) pursuit of those truths that have no bearing upon that which we can *do*. Or we might want to put the accent on subjectivity as the only way to reach the few truths that are open to us in a way that will not result, as Johannes Climacus would say, in an *approximation*. But the idea that truth is whatever you want it to be has got very little to do with Kierkegaard. To some critics, the famous precept may appear trivial on close inspection. But for those determined to uncover the irrational in Kierkegaard, this is probably not the place to look. And indeed, there now seems to be degree of consensus among Kierkegaard scholars about this, whatever his broader reputation might be.[1]

Truth, by being *what is true for you*, then, does not thereby turn into opinion in that last extract (WoL 252–253), but it does come about with help from a subjunctive mood. Its implied premises are assumed in advance of empirical support but the consequences of an advance being granted are unique. These consequences *make up* the truth that had been treated as if it were a ground. Kindness, and especially acts of mercy, may imply propositions about others whose truth can only be stated in the indicative when the other has in fact been built up by mercy. But Kierkegaard's teaching is that only for temporality is there this *order of events*. There is no before and after in eternity, even if eternity's appearance in time has to be like, say, a future. Even religious agnosticism is very welcome to help itself to this much eternity, where 'eternity' *just means*: no before or after. The thought of such a realm should not, at any rate, scandalize anybody who has not also been scandalized by, for example, Kant's first *Critique*, the Eleatics, or indeed, Spinoza.

ii. DESPAIR LEADING INTO HOPE

Despair, though, is a concept that does appear across Kierkegaard's authorship; not just in *The Sickness unto Death*. Often enough, the mentions of despair will be accompanied by a notion of what may lead a person out of despair. And often enough – let us take *Works of Love*, for example – this notion will not presume to show despair as that which should immediately become self-cancelling on being detected, or exposed as having been founded upon a delusion or a wrong-headed way of relating to existence:

> Marvellous words of comfort [. . .] because, humanly speaking, it is indeed most strange, almost like mockery, to say to the despairing person that he *shall* do that which was his sole desire but the impossibility of which brings him to despair. (WoL 42)

This comes from 'You *Shall* Love' and represents an acceptance of despair as understandable, as human and even momentarily appropriate. The 'way out' here is partly a reminder that sorrow can be a task, not just a thing undergone, and partly an upholding of the validity of that which has led to despair; a love, a 'sole desire' in this case. It is as if willingness fully to dwell amidst the determinants of sorrow – and thus, perhaps, to face up to the full seriousness of a predicament – will lead to an appropriation of that which had been despair, such that despair turns back into the love – or something similar to the love – that had occasioned it. It is not that Kierkegaard or any of his pseudonyms give an account that differs from the Anti-Climacus view in respect of the degree to which despair should somehow be *upheld*. But nor is there in a book like *Works of Love*, a sense that all desire can or should be laid down, and that consequently all sorrow will be abandoned. On the contrary:

> I do not have the right to become insensitive to life's pain, because I *shall* sorrow; but neither do I have the right to despair, because I shall sorrow; and neither do I have the right to stop sorrowing, because I *shall* sorrow. (WoL 43)

But Anti-Climacus does view despair as a phenomenon with which he can, as it were, do business. This is because once despair has been revealed as such, it can be dealt with as an orientation of a person's existence. This is in contrast to some of the forms despair may take which, at first glance, call for an examination of the person's thought processes and their *validity*. A great example of this is the way 'doubt' – in the eyes of Johannes Climacus – will so often turn out to be an existential matter, and it is obviously to Johannes Climacus that the author of *Practice in Christianity*, Anti-Climacus, refers when he writes:

> In the work of some pseudonymous writers it has been pointed out that in modern philosophy there is a confused discussion of doubt where the discussion should have been about despair. Therefore one has been unable to control or govern doubt either in scholarship or life. 'Despair,' however, promptly points in the right direction by placing the relation under the rubric of personality (the single individual) and the ethical. (PC 81)

Now when Anti-Climacus tells us that despair 'promptly points in the right direction', he might mean that *discursively* it points our analysis in the right direction. At the same time, though, it could be that despair itself when recognizable by the individual as being despair (rather than being masked by whole range of other emotions, distractions and preoccupations) is said to be pointing the real-life individual in the right direction. And in that case, despair can be said to lead to hope both discursively and in life (potentially). Doubt, at least as an eventuality, was depicted by Johannes Climacus as almost constitutive of consciousness as such, and so perhaps it is a difficult example for Anti-Climacus to have chosen, rather than unmasking, say, grandiosity, dissipation or – as he does in *The Sickness unto Death* – defiance, as despair (although it is an understandable choice given that *Practice* is dealing with the paradox of the Incarnation). Defiance, dissipation, pride, self-hatred and the like are, after all, not ever-present facets of life as Johannes Climacus perceives the menace of doubt to be. But then again, doubt is not too big for despair in Kierkegaard's world; let us not forget what we have read about *the universality of this sickness* (despair) in *The Sickness unto Death*.

In all the talk of universality, though, Kierkegaard does not forget what universality means; it means everybody, not just a rude or unenlightened multitude. Included amongst those for whom despair is constantly lying in wait is none other than the Apostle Paul, Paul who in running has to forget, although he is not running in order to forget – no – because Paul is a penitent as well as being one who runs. In one way Paul's running is what shields him from despair, in another way his running *is* his repentance.

iii. KIERKEGAARD AND PAUL: ROMANS AND CORINTHIANS IN *WORKS OF LOVE*

Although there are references in Kierkegaard's *Works of Love* to St Paul's letters to the Galatians, Ephesians, Philippians and Thessalonians as well as his letters to Timothy, Titus and the Hebrews, we should perhaps limit the discussion here to Romans and Corinthians. This is partly because it is to verses from Romans and Corinthians that Kierkegaard turns when he wants the whole of a 'deliberation' (this is how the chapters are characterized in English translations) to be guided by Paul's teaching. Specifically, 'Love is the fulfilling of the Law', which is the 'A' section of the third deliberation in the first series, elaborates on Romans 13:10, and the fifth of that third series of deliberations, 'Our Duty to Remain in Love's Debt to One Another', is based on Romans 13:8. In the second series, the first, second, third, fourth and sixth deliberations are based on verses from the two letters to the Corinthians. Moreover, while St Paul is everywhere in *Works of Love*, references to Romans and Corinthians are especially numerous across the text as a whole.

St Paul seems to have had a special importance for Kierkegaard. For Kierkegaard, Paul is more than a reference point, more than the embodiment of an idea. Paul comes to life and his life is reported across the pages of Kierkegaard's authorship and not just in *Works of Love*. We see it, for example, in the second of the *Four Upbuilding Discourses* of 1844, entitled 'The Thorn in the Flesh', which responds to Chapter 12 of the Second Letter to the Corinthians and deals with the importance of not dwelling on the sins of the past, not because one is – as we might say today – 'in denial' about them, but because there is work to do. We must keep running, yes, but not away from the recollection of sin, we must run – as Paul did – forward into more work. About Paul, Kierkegaard writes:

> Just as the eye cannot really catch hold of someone who runs, because he is running, so also with sufferings; future sufferings have no time to terrify the apostle, and past sufferings have no time to hold him fast, because he is running. (EUD 332)

Now it could be that the real life of Paul finds its way into Kierkegaard's works purely and simply because to read Paul at all is like being in his company and involved in his activities; in addition to the reflections, rejoicings and entreaties, Paul's letters contain a good deal of information about what he is trying to do, who is helping him, where he has been staying and how it has all been progressing. See, for example, Chapters 15 and 16 of Romans. We also have the Apostle's many salutations and acknowledgements. It is quite normal for a letter to contain salutations to various people, of course. But there is a special magic and a certain charm in the way that all this 'other business' – as it were – is carefully gone through at the end of such profound reflections on human frailty and such bracing ideas about God. You are a Christian in Rome, let us say, and at one moment, Paul is telling you that 'whatsoever is not of faith is sin' – Romans 14:23 – and perhaps thereby being a little bit frightening. But in the next moment he is reassuring you that he will definitely try and get to see you when he finally gets a chance to go to Spain; he will come via you (15:23 and 15:24). It is easy to see how Paul's preaching may have terrified and transfixed its listeners, but it is also easy to see why he may have had so many friends. He is very attentive and caring, he remembers kindnesses done to him and he sends his very best wishes.

So is it just that Paul's own liveliness and charisma has rubbed off on the way Kierkegaard makes use of him? Is that why at moments it feels as if Paul himself is climbing into Kierkegaard's discourse and into his narrations as easily as – if not at points more easily than – Socrates? Is it that you can hardly get hold of Paul without becoming like him, and certainly not if you are as receptive as Kierkegaard – who does become like Socrates when he thinks of Socrates – tends to be? Is it just that Paul's excitement is infectious? Or is it that since Kierkegaard is already a practitioner of the *addressed* communication – whether it be that of prayer or of the discourse addressed to 'that single individual [he] calls [his] reader' – and so feels uniquely drawn to one whose thoughts are conveyed *to* a second person (albeit a second person plural – 'my brethren'), rather than *for* a third person?

Any or all of these factors might be relevant. There is, however, plenty more to it. For there is a deep thematic link, and we might even say that there is a philosophical agreement of sorts. It has something to do with being against the judgment of others. It is something about fearing to judge. It is something about the deadening effect on the spirit that drawing a *conclusion* about another may have. It is something very unworldly indeed. It hits you fulsomely at the start of the second chapter of Romans when Paul says:

> Therefore thou art inexcusable, O man, whosever thou art that judgest: for wherein thou judgest another, thou condemnest thyself, for thou that judgest does the same things.

The criticisms of judging made by Kierkegaard or by Paul himself are not always as sweeping as this. However, what is encouraged throughout *Works of Love* and indeed throughout the Epistles to the Romans and the Corinthians is not only a slowness to judge but a certain slowness to 'realize' – however quietly such realization may 'dawn' – what *other people are like*. Reluctance to 'see' people *in their true colours*, or *as they really are* – this is what is being celebrated. Willingness to recognize that since we are not yet at the end of time we may still be pleasantly surprised by our neighbours – this is being heartily (and in Kierkegaard's case quite methodically) commended to us. Finitude is often imposed artificially by what Kierkegaard calls worldly wisdom (although we might add that to the extent to which the finitude is imposed and thus artificial, it may not even be wise from the point of worldliness). The thoughts that we have about others should always be in some sense *unfinished*. And who better than St Paul to raise up the possibility that all may change in the next moment, given what we know about his own past? 'For I am the least of the apostles' says Paul in Corinthians (15:9), 'that am not meet to be called an apostle, because I persecuted the church of God'.

Naturally, such hopeful or, if you will, 'unfinished' thoughts about others will not always arrive nor be sustained very easily when a person is in the thick of life or the heat of the moment – Kierkegaard is more than ready to admit as much. It may sometimes be a tall order to keep our thoughts about one another *unfinished*. We may have learned to remind ourselves how little we know even if we know a fair deal. But unless that lesson is constantly put into practice, we may well still return to our old ways of judging, dismissing, condemning or at least *concluding*; we may well be like Kierkegaard's dog, at the end of 'Love Believes All Things' (WoL 244), who can learn to walk upright for a while but soon wants to go back to walking on all fours. But managing this tall order may have some consolations, if not some practical advantages. Let us think a little bit more about this.

George Eliot observes in her all-too-frequently-overlooked novel *Silas Marner*, that noble souls unschooled in the suspicion of others, unacquainted with the processes of malicious thinking and wholly disposed to see no evil may be driven almost to the edge of insanity when cornered by some horrid betrayal (of the sort experienced by one of the main characters in that story). The suggestion is that what the world at large might view as an overreaction to a piece of shabby behaviour arises – and this is the awful pathos of the situation and perhaps its tragic dimension – because the sufferer of the betrayal has no bearings, no familiar paths, has been catapulted up over an uncharted ocean, and is in free-fall: 'Poor Marner went out with that despair in his soul – that shaken trust in God and man, which is little short of madness to a loving nature.'[2]

Bitterness and resentment may flood into such a soul, not because the soul was already inclined towards those emotions, but rather because, having no propensity for them, that soul has no flood defences in place. In the turmoil, the wounded party is completely consumed by the injury, is devoured by the hatred that a more worldly character would experience – yes indeed – but hatred that a more worldly personality would have also prudently managed to keep in its place to a degree. The innocent, on the other hand, has not seen it coming and is knocked for six. Hatred not only of the immediate offender but of all those rallying to his or her side and then, by extension, to all of humanity, perhaps precisely because no section of humanity, nor even perhaps any whole person, had previously been supposed malevolent – this is the horrid irony of the whole affair – quickly ensues.

Now, it will probably be quite impossible for those who do know the story of *Silas Marner* to think of a way in which the perpetrator of the betrayal in question could somehow be acquitted. But imagine a scenario in which a betrayal or an apparent betrayal had that effect of plunging its victim into near-madness but where there was a tiny chink of a possibility that the whole situation had been misread. (Indeed, the physiognomy of Silas Marner himself is misunderstood by the local boys who would come round bothering him from time to time: malevolent powers are ascribed to an apparent harshness of facial expression that is really due to short-sightedness.[3]) A few paragraphs back, we thought about a tall order that might nevertheless have its consolations, if not its advantages. Would not the afflicted soul reach out for the challenge of that tall order (the tall order of leaving thoughts about the other person unfinished), especially if the alternative was total derangement, in the way that a sick person reaches out for a cordial? Would it not be that far from the dog walking on hind legs being the image for the Christian humility that is ready to believe only the good but that is hard to maintain, the grasping at that chink of possibility and the reaching out for thoughts that are unfinished would be more close to what the dog feels when returning to four legs? Kierkegaard usually writes about the ordinary person who is prone to see the worst and will rarely give the benefit of the doubt, as if doing the opposite (that is to say – assuming good intentions on the part of the other) is what requires more energy. Perhaps, however, the energy required is no more than a *burst* of energy at the point of *transition* from the nightmare of a thousand finished thoughts and supposedly inescapable conclusions to the sunlit uplands of thoughts about others or about another that are, fortunately and – in more than one sense – mercifully incomplete.

St Paul does almost seem to hint at this. It is almost with a sense of relief that he teaches and that we read that only God can judge. Hugh Pyper has drawn attention[4] to the following passage in Romans (12:19):

> Dearly beloved, avenge not yourselves, but rather give place unto wrath: for it is written, Vengeance is mine; I will repay, saith the Lord.

That said, Paul does warn the Corinthians not only that he will be visiting soon to do some serious judging but that he has already judged the authors of certain deeds from afar (see 1 Corinthians 5). Then again, it is, of course, in Chapter 13 of 1 Corinthians that we find all those amazing verses that Kierkegaard takes as his inspiration for Part II of his *Works of Love*. Let us have a look at what is concerning Kierkegaard in the deliberation entitled 'Love Hopes All Things – and Yet Is Never Put to Shame' (WoL 249).

Now Constantin Constantius in the course of his 'Venture in Experimenting Psychology' (Kierkegaard's *Repetition*) depicts hope as a sort of confinement. But elsewhere in Kierkegaard 'hope' is richer than this. It may even be that the Kierkegaardian idea of *the love that hopes all things* contains something of Constantin's 'repetition', for all Constantin himself may distinguish and contrast the latter with hope (FT/R 132). But at any rate, one way in which hope can be richer is when it is the hope for other people. This is Kierkegaard imagining what hope (personified) would reply to despair's attempt to talk a person into trusting no-one, since anybody at all could eventually let you down.

> Yes, it certainly is possible, but then the opposite is also possible. 'Therefore never unlovingly give up hope on any human being or give up hope for that person, since it is possible that even the most prodigal son could be saved, that even the most embittered enemy—alas—he who was your friend—it is possible that he could again become your friend. It is possible that one who sank the deepest—alas, because he stood so high—it is possible that he

> could again be raised up. It is still possible that the love that became cold could again begin to burn. Therefore never give up on any human being; do not despair, not even at the last moment—no, hope all things.' (WoL 254)

Kierkegaard goes on to argue that one only truly hopes for oneself when one also has hope for others. His reasoning could be linked back to the 'Purity of Heart' ideas that we discussed at the end of the Chapter 2. To hope for something – if it really is only *one thing* for which one hopes – is necessarily to hope for *the good*. And here in 'Love Hope All Things – and Yet Is Never Put to Shame' Kierkegaard refers to the idea that 'the good has an infinite connectedness' as part of his explanation of why truly to hope is to hope for others as for oneself.

> No one can hope unless he is also loving; he cannot *hope for himself* without also being loving, because the good has an infinite connectedness; but if he is loving, he also hopes for others. (WoL 255)

In the next and last chapter we will perhaps be quite close to this idea when we explore one or two ideas about what 'community' and also 'democracy' could involve when we have the philosophy of Søren Kierkegaard at our disposal.

CHAPTER 6

HIS CONTINUING RELEVANCE: COMMUNITY AND THE INDIVIDUAL

i. THE IMPENITENT CROWD

Certain aspects of Kierkegaard's outlook appear to undergo degrees of change across the authorship. We have discussed a few of these already, and there are one or two more for us to look at in this last chapter. However, there are many themes that endure with hardly a sign of variation. One of these is the theme of *the crowd* – that ungraspable, irresponsible, perhaps even *unconscious* agency that eats up individuals and wields immense power, yet cannot be held to account. We can call 'the crowd' a theme as easily as we might call it a concept, because in Kierkegaard there is a sensitivity to all sorts of phenomena – linguistic usages, say, or prevalent but unexplored assumptions – that have potentially crowd-like dimensions or properties; 'the crowd' is thematically operative throughout Kierkegaard's writings.

Significantly, the crowd will appear in Kierkegaard as 'impenitent' (WoL 169). We know that a crowd can be 'impenitent' when its assaults upon a given target are relentless – remorseless, indeed. We know how crowd behaviour can acquire a momentum of its own and produce unintended and even unforeseeable consequences for which no individual can be held answerable. In Kierkegaard, a crowd can be 'impenitent' because it has the bewildering ability to vanish suddenly, to appear to have existed nowhere, as it were, or to have no particular members (see for example, UDVS 131), or perhaps only a few reluctant or habitual subscribers who – perhaps in all sincerity – do not really *subscribe* at all to what the crowd is doing right at this moment:

> And the public will be unrepentant, for it actually does not keep the dog, it merely subscribes; neither did it directly goad the dog

> to attack nor whistle it back. In the event of a lawsuit, the public would say: The dog is not mine; the dog has no owner. And if the dog is apprehended and sent to the school of veterinary medicine to be exterminated, the pubic could still say: It was really a good thing that the bad dog was exterminated; we all wanted it done—even the subscribers. (TA 95)

On one hand the issue is that an accused person, or several accused people, can take cover in a crowd. They can hide from each other, from the authorities, and even from themselves perhaps, when there is a crowd in sight. We have seen this happen enough times in the movies. (Sometimes it is only a case of a protagonist needing to take temporary shelter in crowd while working out how to prove his or her innocence and sometimes the technique will be adopted by a real baddy.) Kierkegaard suspects that crowds attract that sort of participant. Indeed, he proposes that from a strictly religious point of view all the members of the human race are at constant risk of behaving like those 'few' guilty ones.

> When out of seven people who are all charged with having committed a crime others could not have committed, the seventh says, 'It was not I, it was the others,' 'the others' are understood to be the six others, and so on down the line. But what if all seven, each one separately, said, 'It was the others'?—what then? Does that not conjure up a mirage that has multiplied the actual seven in an attempt to fool us into thinking that there were many more, although there were only seven? So, too, when the whole human race, each one separately, hits upon saying 'the others,' an apparition is conjured up, as if the race existed one more time in addition to the time of its actual existence, except that it is very difficult here to point out the falsity, the bedazzlement with the appearance of profundity, because the race is innumerable. (WoL 116–117)

On the other hand, Kierkegaard's concern is that there is, in society, a kind of monster, a gigantic monster made out of nothingness – the *public*. Some of Kierkegaard's thoughts about *the public* can be separated out from his consideration of the crowd as an entity in which one may merely hide or try to hide. It might be that the sort of crowd or crowding with which Kierkegaard associates what he calls *the public* is much more perplexing to him and more sinister.

The mere scoundrel who seeks the cover of a crowd is at least retaining, after all, a measure of self-definition as, precisely, a fugitive. Consciousness of guilt could, in principle, emerge from the very self-recognition that may initially have been required for the securing of a successful get-away. Dialectically – we can almost hear Kierkegaard saying – there is some hope for such a one in respect of the religious. Individuality is still potentially visible the case of the crowd that shelters an accused. Discursively, the individual can appear first, and then, lo and behold, there is the issue of how that individual may abscond, or pass the buck, and so forth, and so we can then talk about the crowd, and this is broadly the shape of the above-quoted extract. But when it comes to *the public*, what is terrifying is that you do not even have a villain, or a collection of villains, on the run:

> The public is not a people, not a generation, not one's age, not a congregation, not association, not some particular persons, for all these are what they are only by being concretions. Yes, not a single one of these who belong to a public is essentially engaged in any way. For a few hours of the day he perhaps is part of the public, that is, during the hours when he is a nobody, because during the hours in which he is the specific person he is, he does not belong to the public. (TA 93)

There is a real-life pathos in the scenario Kierkegaard invokes that results from his mention of the *hours* that are in a day; amidst the abstraction of his essay he places these *hours*, and straightaway we have a sense of this all being *real*, and real on a daily basis. We will be imagining, perhaps, a more or less decent sort of person, a sinner of sorts, maybe, but by no means a monster, returning home and finding those hours in which *somebody* starts to come to life. But what of the other hours – the hours when 'nobody' was home? In *those* hours, inactivity is possible, including the sort of inactivity that might be deemed reprehensible in another context – the context of an individual being present, say. In *those* hours, activity is also possible, but as a sort of allied sleepwalking – so that the credit or the culpability that would otherwise attach to an individual in connection with actions completed will appear only as curious abstractions, if they appear at all. In *those* hours, it can also be observed, subjectivity may congratulate itself as it forms opinions on vital matters, feels nothing but contempt for such and such a politician, is downright indignant about this recently announced policy and *hopping mad* about that one. Of course we would hope that all these emotions and thoughts and could also be experienced and undertaken by the specific person in the hours when he or she 'does not belong to the public' and of course Kierkegaard would want us to think about what types of seriousness and what types of isolation would be required in order to ensure that *now* we do indeed have a single individual behind the considered opinion, say, or the indignation, or the being-hopping-mad and so on and so forth.

The troubling complexity of the whole affair is that even when we sit at home in armchairs or on our own, there is no guarantee that we will have set aside the hours when we belong to *the public* instead of to ourselves, if we will grant Kierkegaard that distinction, for all it may ultimately be, to the extent that it is meant to reflect a reality, a religiously rooted one. (If it is a purely a distinction in rhetoric, then perhaps we can grant it to him *as a piece of existentialism*). In a culture and at a time where *having your say* is considered a terribly good thing – more, in fact, than it was ever considered to be in Kierkegaard's time and in his *milieu* – we should probably all watch out for the temptation to recline wisely in our powerless importance as we award the politicians marks. We should be careful about settling too comfortably into the superiority of being the electorate – the customer who is always right – while they, the potentates, effectively egg us on in this cosy dream by answering the supposedly penetrating interviewers like sheepish schoolboys hoping that the telling-off will end soon. Let us not flatter ourselves:

> The category 'public' is reflection's mirage delusively making the individuals conceited, since everyone can arrogate to himself this mammoth, compared to which the concretions of actuality seem paltry. The public is the fairy tale in an age of prudence, leading individuals to fancy themselves greater than kings [. . .]. (TA 93)

Now at the same time, Kierkegaard observes, there is, in an age of reflection in contrast with what he calls an age of revolution, a marked tendency to back off from any engagement that would pin an individual to 'an idea' with all the associated risks to security and status. And this is linked to yet another way in which *the public* is impenitent, and can legitimately shrug off any suggestion that it should be anything other than impenitent:

> The established order continues to stand, but since it is equivocal and ambiguous, passionless reflection is assured. We do not want to abolish the monarchy, by no means, but if little by little we could get it transformed into make-believe, we would gladly shout 'Hurrah for the King!' We do not want to topple eminence, by no means, but if simultaneously we could spread the notion that it is all make-believe, we would approve and admire. In the same way we are willing to keep Christian terminology but privately know that nothing decisive is supposed to be meant by it. And we will not be repentant, for after all we are not demolishing anything. (TA 80–81)

This is one of the ways that Kierkegaard characterizes what he calls 'the present age'. But of course there is a tension – often an ironically remarked-upon tension – in Kierkegaard's writings over his own attitude to the age in which he himself lived. In one moment of his thought Kierkegaard – with his frequently occurring satire at the expense of 'what the times demand' – finds it suspect and faintly preposterous that 'an age' should be able to see itself as fundamentally distinguishable in any way; it is perhaps a short step from there to a thought than an age is somehow not just distinguishable but *distinguished* – sophisticated, advanced and the like – by comparison with all others. This will strike him as potentially absurd when the distinguishing factors are contingent, and yet then again, how could the factors ever be otherwise? For if they are not so, then it is hardly *an age* that is being discerned at all. So in another moment of Kierkegaard's thinking, he does look for the propensities of a time, and even if he is then able to fly off, or at least step back, and make 'the age' a mere motif for a phenomenon that could in fact appear in any merely historical age, it cannot be forgotten that a notion has emerged from the diagnosis of a particular time; it is immediately a characterization of one time rather than another. If 'the crowd' is especially impenitent,[1] if 'the public' is especially anonymous in an age of reflection, we cannot help but hold him to the implication that he has started with a point in history, and any comparisons of, say the mid-nineteenth century in Copenhagen with our own time will have to be just that, comparisons of two periods of time, as opposed to general insights into the human condition. And then, understandably, we will want to know what Kierkegaard thinks of a contrasting age. This brings us, of course, to what he calls *the age of revolution*. What he says about the age of revolution may be surprising to some, especially those who are more aware of the conservative tendencies in Kierkegaard.

ii. INDIVIDUALS AND 'THE IDEA'

Anyone could be forgiven for supposing that Kierkegaard, with his reservations about 'worldly' forms of emancipation and his notable pessimism in respect of collective attempts to make progress in this life, would have misgivings and only misgivings about an *age of revolution*. Oddly enough, however, and notwithstanding the fact that Kierkegaard would scarcely want to be identified as a supporter of any revolution, his remarks about what an 'age of revolution' can do to consciousness are not wholly critical – far from it, in fact. If anything, we can see a stage-like or sphere-like hierarchy emerging in which 'the age of reflection' is a lower sphere than 'the age of revolution' which, while it may not be a candidate for the highest form of life, possesses attributes that are appealing to Kierkegaard, and most notably, the sense in which individuals persist in being separated *as* individuals when what unites them is *an idea*. Some of the things Kierkegaard says will strike us perhaps a little bit strange, especially with the whole history of the twentieth century lying between him and us, but they are though-provoking nevertheless:

> The age of revolution is essentially passionate; therefore it must be able to be violent, riotous, wild, ruthless toward everything but its idea, but precisely because it still has one motivation, it is less open to the charge of *crudeness*. (TA 62)

Surely, we might counter, there is no contest between a society in which we have to endure *crudeness* and one in which there is out-and-out violence and ruthlessness, no matter how high-minded the motivation? Moreover, we could presumably refer him, were he here to debate the matter with us, to examples of supposedly revolutionary cultures in which all the behaviours he ascribes to his concept of 'the public' are very much in evidence, not excepting *crudeness*. Well, it could be that Kierkegaard would agree wholeheartedly. But it could also be that without in any sense *recommending* any real move into a revolutionary age, Kierkegaard is, almost as a kind of thought experiment, outlining the virtues of such an age in connection with what to him is the most important category – and he frequently does call it a category – the category of 'the individual'.

> Where individuals (each one individually) are essentially and passionately related to an idea and together are essentially related to the same idea, the relation is optimal and normative. Individually the relation separates them (each one has himself for himself), and ideally it unites them. Where there is essential inwardness, there is decent modesty between man and man that prevents crude aggressiveness; in the relation of unanimity to the idea there is the elevation that again in consideration of the whole forgets the accidentality of details. Thus the individuals never come to close to each other in the herd sense, simply because they are united on the basis of an ideal distance. The unanimity of separation is indeed fully orchestrated music. On the other hand, if individuals relate to an idea *en masse* (consequently without the individual separation of inwardness), we get violence, anarchy, riotousness; but if there is no idea for the individuals *en masse* and no individually separating essential inwardness, either, then we have crudeness. (TA 62–63)

Here it becomes more apparent, perhaps, that Kierkegaard is not extolling the virtues of revolution so much as negatively demonstrating the need of his 'present age' – which he terms an age of reflection, for *an idea*. The implication is that *an idea*, were it combined with the 'individually separating essential inwardness' – though this is arguably quite a provisional, if not fairly nebulous formulation – would throw up a society that was preferable to both the present age and the age of revolution. Shortly after this, Kierkegaard says that if we 'remove the relation to oneself' we will get 'the tumultuous self-relating of the mass to an idea' but that if we 'remove this [that is: the idea] as well' we will have 'crudeness' (TA 63). We have a clear indication here that a hierarchy has been constructed in his mind. This is almost certainly not meant to be construed as a hierarchy of what is preferable, but rather a hierarchy that measures nothing more and nothing less than what the different ages *have*. The revolutionary age is missing significant elements necessary for what a human life should be, but the present age – which he now practically starts to *call* 'crudeness' – *has* even less.

It certainly seems that Kierkegaard is prepared to entertain one or two quasi-romantic perspectives on the idea of the revolutionary age and, somewhat paradoxically, they often come close to evincing that nostalgia for bygone days of heroic action and grand consequences that some would identify as the hallmark of a certain *conservative* sensibility: 'The immediacy of the age of revolution is a restoring of natural relationships in contrast to a fossilized formalism which, by having lost the originality of the ethical, has become a dessicated ruin, a narrow-hearted custom and practice' (TA 65). On the whole, however, his preoccupation is with what he wants to set in contrast to that vision (and with this in mind it may be significant that the section of *Two Ages* entitled 'The Age of Revolution' is much shorter than the section entitled 'The Present Age'), and he depicts that *even lower* form of life most evocatively: 'Individuals do not in inwardness turn away from each other, do not turn outward in unanimity for an idea, but mutually turn to each other in a frustrating and suspicious, aggressive, levelling reciprocity' (TA 63).

iii. KIERKEGAARD VERSUS THE HERD

While it may seem that the Dane fancies that there would be slightly more hope of meeting individuals in a revolutionary age, are we sure that in a dull passionless age (not only dominated by the masses but dominated by masses without 'an idea') there would not be an occasion, in Kierkegaard's eyes, for single individuals to be awoken? The notion of such an awakening, an awakening prompted by the need for some opposition, is exactly the sort notion that Kierkegaard – in this respect an unswerving devotee of the dialectical – would want to countenance. Now although Kierkegaard does not explicitly mention democracy in the passages discussed above, it has sometimes been concluded that his remarks about 'the public' and his laments about 'levelling' are signs of a soul ill-at-ease, almost in exile, in what is experienced as a increasingly swampy world of undifferentiated 'nobodies'[2] that have gradually come to hold sway as a consequence of what we today might recognize as democratic progress. However, there are those who contend that it is precisely because of a need to transcend or stand in defiance of various forms of stifling herd mentality that Kierkegaard welcomes the democratic age as the difficult ground upon which true individuality can emerge and be tested, and the passage that is often adduced in this connection reads as follows:

> But if the individual is not destroyed in the process, he will be educated by this very abstraction and this abstract discipline (insofar as he is not already educated in his own inwardness) to be satisfied in the highest religious sense with himself and his relationship to God, will be educated to make up his own mind instead of agreeing with the public, which annihilates all the relative concretions of individuality, to find rest within himself, at ease before God, instead of counting and counting. (TA 92)

It might be slightly optimistic to cite this passage as an indication of Kierkegaard's eventual willingness to welcome a more democratic age. It is not that the Dane is not in some sense welcoming the advent of such an age, to be fair. But Kierkegaard is counterpoising contentment – 'in the highest religious sense' – with self and with a God-relationship to the democratic age in a dialectical way. His logic is not dissimilar to the logic he would use to show that various kinds of hardship can be transformed into blessings if they are accepted as gifts from God. It is not entirely clear that Kierkegaard has reasons beyond the schooling of the individual – 'if he does not succumb in the process' – for thinking that the abstraction of the age is to be welcomed. It may be up to us, and specifically up to thinkers like Alastair Hannay, to show how the one who has been 'educated to find peace with himself and with God' could then, as it were, 'return' to society and participate more effectively, and as a more intelligently inspired player, in any struggle for the betterment of humanity. And this is so even if 'the betterment of humanity' is understood as Kierkegaard would want it understood, bearing in mind his remarks about the only true help for another person being help that would in some way lead him or her to the God-relation, but not in any way that would compromise the independence of the one helped – hence the repeated emphasis in *Two Ages* on the idea that the truest and best helpers in a new and better society would be *unrecognizable*. Alastair Hannay writes:

> The prompting cannot, therefore, take the form of direct assistance, advice, or instruction, for that would be to deprive others of their autonomy and so amount to the dereliction of the leader's role; it would be to 'dabble in the shortsighted ingenuity of human sympathy', and thereby precisely to *prevent* others from

> making the freedom-constituting link themselves. Kierkegaard refers to the new leaders as 'the unrecognizable' (*Ukjendelige*).[3]

However, it would not necessarily be to read against Kierkegaard to start exploring those ideas about a 'returning' individual being a more inspired and effective participant in some form of social struggle, given that Kierkegaard does not even give detailed projections of how the betterment of humanity as he *does* conceive it could be accomplished. So are we then saying that we can start, without seriously contradicting him, to use Kierkegaard's thought to guess at how the single individual can act for the betterment of humanity as Kierkegaard does *not* conceive it? Well, not to put too fine a point on the matter: yes, quite possibly we can, and maybe we should. Why should we? Is it because we simply would like to be decent, pleasant and hopeful about all things and thus to be spending time only on philosophy that has (dare we say it?) *outcomes and deliverables* – whether or not we are religious? Is it that that we do not want to find ourselves, if we are not religious (or not religious in Kierkegaard's way) at a dead-end with *such a great and captivating thinker* as Kierkegaard? Is it that we cannot bear to have been so compelled by his thought and taken with his themes and yet also discover that this thought and these themes may not all add up to anything that *in this world* would count as *a good thing*? Well, maybe or maybe not. But if we really do want to cleave only to what Kierkegaard actually stated, and to eschew attempts to gather possible implications for the good of society from his work, then consistency requires that we follow him all the way and face up to how he actually did conclude. And are we prepared for that? Do we know what it is? Well, this book is here to provide information about what it is, and so it will do just that in the following section.

iv. DENMARK'S A PRISON

> *Ham.* [. . .] Let me question more in particular: what have you, my good friends, deserved at the hands of fortune that she sends you to prison hither?
>
> *Guil.* Prison, my lord?
>
> *Ham.* Denmark's a prison.
>
> *Ros.* Then is the world one.
>
> *Ham.* A goodly one; in which there are many confines, wards, and dungeons, Denmark being one of the worst.

It is a frequently overlooked fact that Kierkegaard repeatedly concluded – in various journal entries from the 1850s – that the only real betterment of humanity would be for humanity to disappear altogether. Perhaps this is not surprising from one who repeatedly called existence a prison.[4] He believed, in the end, that marriage and especially procreation was wrong. With the Paul's letters in mind, and also, we may surmise, all that is implied by the definitions of purity that we find in The Book of Revelations, Kierkegaard spells it out: 'Christianity teaches that the propagation of the species is a mistake' (LY 288). A mistake for all Christians, and he wanted all to be Christians, so let us just say: *a mistake*.

> The error in Catholicism is not that the priest is celibate; no, the error is that a qualitative difference between the layman and the priest has been introduced, which goes clean against the New Testament, and is a concession of weakness in relation to numbers. Certainly the error is not that the priest is a celibate—a Christian should be celibate. (LY 264)

It should be understood, moreover, that these statements do not appear to be 'off-the-cuff' or part of a mere thought experiment, and if they emerge from what Kierkegaard himself might call a 'mere mood' of pessimism, then it must be recognized that Kierkegaard pursues the theme over many journal entries, pessimistically or otherwise, and elaborates it from a range of different angles. On one hand, we have the appeal to the sheer misery of this existence and the inescapability of it for the poor child born into it, the child who may well ask for an explanation:

> When [a man] at last reaches maturity, and if his view of life is the Christian, then it could surely never occur to him to want to give life to a child. To give life to a child! A child is born in sin, having been conceived in transgression, and this existence is a vale of tears—is that what you will tell your child, will this give you openness towards the child that owes its existence to you? (LY 264)

On the other hand, we have Kierkegaard's attempt at what could be called a God's-eye perspective, in which the issue is the pity God might have for humanity, yes, but also God's wish to 'pick a quarrel' with humanity over the endless renewals of sin and sinfulness, with the appearance of Christianity being the very opposition to human existence and its 'fall away from [God]' (LY 270–271), its 'false step' (LY 271). With the directness that is so characteristic of the later Kierkegaard, he puts the conjecture like this:

> That is what Christianity is for—which straightaway bars the way to procreation. This means: stop! I have put up long enough with this world historical process, certainly I will have pity, but I do not want any more of the consequences of that false step. (LY 271)

If we believe that all marriage and reproduction are wrong, we hold a view that ought to be taken seriously, one that should receive more careful consideration than it is likely to attract any time soon.[5] Moreover, this view would not exclude us from the *option* of thinking that in addition, ideas about community and love for the neighbour can be inspired by Kierkegaard in ways he did not quite foresee or intend. However, if we do not believe that the species ought to expire, then can we dismiss attempts to show Kierkegaard's *potential* contributions to theories of social action on the basis that this would be a move away from what he actually said? What he *did* say, after all, is that procreation ought to cease. Now perhaps we *are* willing to take that as the genuine and logical culmination of his thought. And we may or may not dislike the philosophy of Søren Kierkegaard for it. However, if we do *not* see a moral requirement upon us all to desist from reproducing as being the most logical culmination of Kierkegaard's thought, or at least if we do not see it as the culmination that does most justice to the spirit of his work as a whole, then we have no option but to look a little bit beyond *what he actually said* to find an alternative ending.

When Kierkegaard wrote as he did in the above-quoted extracts about the ideal future for humans on this earth (the ideal of their non-existence), he was, we must remember, writing in his journal, a place where all sorts of thoughts would be rehearsed. Even if much of what he says here about the evil of reproduction *is* one of the logical conclusions of much of his earlier work (we might think, for example, of his emphasis upon the importance of *dying to the world*), it could be that this was a conclusion that struck *him* rather abruptly.[6] This may explain the rather shrill manner of exposition, although his thinking was generally less dialectical and he was less of a practitioner of 'indirect communication' in those last years of his life. But however understandable this particular culmination of Kierkegaard's thought might be, we will not necessarily clash with what he propounds in this altogether starker phase of his authorship if we do look for that 'alternative ending' by angling the instruments of his philosophy towards the social, putting his thought about the individual at the disposal of a social consideration. Moreover, if we add to these reflections the fact that many eminent scholars, and Alastair Hannay in particular, have considered that Kierkegaard offered plenty in the way of reflection upon kinder and fairer forms of society,[7] we need not start with an assumption that our pursuit of an 'alternative ending' must inevitably turn Kierkegaard into a different sort of thinker from the one he actually was. Hannay writes:

> But in any case, what cannot be doubted is that Kierkegaard envisages, in however vague a way, a total community in which generally accepted social ideals such as freedom and justice are achieved. It seems true, nevertheless, and consistent with the Kantianism pervading Kierkegaard's ethics, to say that his thinking is concentrated on the conditions in which the end-state can be 'expressed' in the single individual's life, in anticipation of it, as it were, rather than on the details of the end-state itself or on how its expression in the individual's life can in fact contribute causally to its eventual realization.[8]

Besides, as we have indicated, it is not as if believing that the ideal scenario for humans would be their non-existence precludes an interest in maximizing their welfare for the time that they do inhabit the earth. So what kind of thinker, politically viewed, was Kierkegaard? And, assuming that we can get idea of this, where might we then want to take his thought?

v. KIERKEGAARD: CONSERVATIVE REVOLUTIONARY

With the idea in mind that philosophy, having scaled the heights and perhaps penetrated a few of the mysteries, will often *leave everything as it is*, we could perhaps think of Søren Aabye Kierkegaard as a kind of *conservative revolutionary*. It is odd that Kierkegaard, in *The Present Age*, maintained that his was purely an age of reflection:

> In contrast to the age of revolution, which took action, the present age is an age of publicity, the age of miscellaneous announcements: nothing happens but still there is instant publicity. An insurrection in this day and age is utterly unimaginable; such a manifestation of power would seem ridiculous to the calculating sensibleness of the age. However, a political virtuoso might be able to perform an amazing tour de force of quite another kind. He would issue invitations to a general meeting for the purpose of deciding on a revolution, wording the invitation so cautiously that even the censor would have to let it pass. On the evening of the meeting, he would so skilfully create the illusion that they had made a revolution that everyone would go home quietly, having passed a very pleasant evening. (TA 70)

But the fact of the matter is Kierkegaard actually *did* live in an age of revolutions. In France, for example, there had been a revolution in 1830 and there was about to be one in 1848, only a year or two after the appearance of the text containing the above remarks. So perhaps he was just talking about Denmark? But then again, possibly not, since we know that Denmark was also to be affected:

> In the year 1848 much of Europe teetered on the edge of revolution. Denmark was involved in a war with Germany, and crowds of 15,000 roamed the streets of Copenhagen. Kierkegaard's response was to complain that his faithful Anders had been drafted into the army just when he was needed, that his stocks had declined 700 rd., and that the turbulence would prevent him from taking a foreign tour.[9]

It seems likely that for all the vehemence, ardour and rhetorical exuberance of Kierkegaard's reflections on the condition of his age, the revolution Kierkegaard seeks to bring about involves no barricades, no charging or storming of any public buildings, nor any cobblestones being dug up and hurled. For all Kierkegaard's disgust and frustration at a smug complacency that he explicitly characterizes as bourgeois, he was by temperament a conservative. He thought radical upheavals achieved little and amounted to nothing but distraction from what he took to be the serious business of life: the transformation of inwardness.

Kierkegaard, whose doctoral dissertation was written in the same year as that of Karl Marx (1841), was a revolutionary – yes, in some ways perhaps he was. Kierkegaard, whose *Works of Love* (*Kjerlighedens Gjerninger*) contains a glance at the crowded dwelling that is not cramped if love is present[10] was published in 1847, just after the Irish potato famine is thought to have gone through its worst and most horrifying phase,[11] may have nevertheless been a kind of revolutionary – in his own strange way. Kierkegaard, who composed *Practice in Christianity* (*Indøvelse i Christendom*), and *The Sickness unto Death* (*Sygdommen til Døden*) in the year of *The Communist Manifesto* (*Das Manifest der Kommunistischen Partei*) – 1848 – this Kierkegaard, like Marx, was arguably *all for revolution*. The revolution he looked for, however, was a revolution in the consciousness of every human. We can almost imagine him out and about on the streets of Copenhagen peering into the faces of those he would meet in search of a sign of this latter kind of revolution (perhaps even holding up a lantern in broad daylight as we are told Diogenes did when he went around looking for *an honest man*), and then continuing on his walk, having been ironic at his own expense and, as it were, joking with himself, that anyone could hope to gain a clue from that kind of observation.

vi. FAITH IN OTHERS AS A BASIS

We usually look at the concept of faith in the context of human beings having it, lacking it or being on their way towards it. However, perhaps we can imagine a conversation in which God's faith in us was the focus. In order to get along we often have to put faith in one another, and alas, we are often disappointed. At this point, we might feel that *our faith was misplaced*. But if we regularly imagined how many times God's faith in us, were he looking down at us, would have to be restored or restarted even over the course of a single day, we might be a little bit more reluctant to operate a three-strikes-and-out policy with our neighbours near and far. This new hardiness in the faith we place in others might count for something.[12] And it might really be something, because Kierkegaard may not necessarily be right to think that true faith has to abandon all expectation of satisfaction in this world. Over time, after all, a climate of forgiveness and generous expectancy may result from the endlessly 'ill-advised' renewals of faith. We are only human, unfortunately, and it is always easier, so much easier, to be kind if one has experienced just a little bit of kindness oneself. Perhaps that is a rather shabby state of affairs, that kindness should be so conditioned. But it is the state of affairs with which we would be *well-advised* to reckon.

There is a clear sense that God is an all-or-nothing issue in Kierkegaard. But if, for some humans, 'God' simply means self-examination, perhaps that does, again, count for something. When we feel righteously embattled or when we feel indignantly wronged, our supposed innocence is so often a calculation of what others ought to feel in relation to us on the basis of what *we* know *they* can see. But if, instead of this, we imagined what God would be able to see in us, even just on the basis of what we know about ourselves – and is it not very much the case that we *do not know the half*? – then perhaps we would, in that humble *imitation* of Godliness whose importance Kierkegaard so forcefully underlined as being central to Christianity, become slower to chide and swifter to bless. Kierkegaard's frustration at the failure of his age to take seriously the *Imitatio Christi* part of religiousness is everywhere apparent. This frustration is summed up when Kierkegaard writes, for example: 'If a person has ethical powers, people will gladly make a genius of him just to be rid of him, for his life contains a demand' (PJS 212). (One of the Kierkegaard scholars who has given a great deal of thought to, and provided detailed discussion of, the notion of exemplarity over a number of years, is John Lippitt.[13])

Slowness to chide, swiftness to bless, willingness to have faith in other people, even after there has been disappointment, these may be qualities which, with *Works of Love* in mind, we could develop in ourselves. Then perhaps, a whole climate has a chance to evolve in which hospitality, responsibility for and renewable faith in others begin to strike us as quite normal. Here we may appear to be taking *Works of Love* away somewhat from the Kierkegaard *we know so well*. He, after all does not want to look at any *climate*. Ah, but perhaps it is precisely single individuals that are required here. Besides, it could be that the humanitarian implications of the non-pseudonymous *Works of Love* should be permitted to fly up and away from the author's own pessimism about *the external*, just as it is understood – or at least just as Kierkegaard wanted it to be understood (for example, in 'The First and Last Declaration') – that the pseudonyms did not speak for him. The deliberate cultivation of certain habits of thought and certain ways of perceiving others might not be heroic. Indeed, once people have succeeded in making such thought processes and ways of perceiving habitual, we may not even be able to keep speaking of virtue, at least according to some accounts of virtue. But there seems to be no reason to suppose that such cultivations – such training in hospitality (including *difficult* hospitality), such schooling in responsibility (including *difficult* responsibility) – are not cultivations with which *single individuals* can edge towards a society in which more people come to less harm. The unimaginable catastrophe of the potato famine – to stay with that example from the time of Kierkegaard's *Works of Love* – might perhaps have been lessened if those with the power to assist had operated not as heroes, nor as great nineteenth century *exceptions* but as upholders of a climate of basic decency in which the abject destitution of others was not to be considered as the sole responsibility of those others. This, as opposed to the idea, lamentably prevalent in the middle of the nineteenth century and beyond, that Ireland should have somehow pulled itself together, or that it might have at least learned some tough but valuable lessons, and other such offensive nonsense.

To the idea of cultivating *a climate* where showing trust and practising hospitality seem normal it might be objected by a Kierkegaardian that good behaviour is being made too 'easy'. But if the aim of ethics is to see that fewer people encounter misery and affliction, then it does not matter whether the way was easy or whether it was hard. If, on the other hand, the aim is to see that everybody has to undergo what we might call the 'personal development challenge' of being good under the harshest conditions, then ethics is no longer what we are discussing, or at least, not in any straightforward way. We would then be discussing individual progress, or perhaps mystical self-denial, or possibly even a certain sort of aesthetic excursion – aesthetic in the *Either/Or* (*Enten–Eller*) sense of the term; the artistic treatment of one's own existence.

This is what could be put to a Kierkegaardian. Would we need to put it to Kierkegaard himself? Perhaps, but let us not assume that Kierkegaard was always turned in on the perfecting of charitable motives over and above a *focus* on consequences (however pessimistic about the consequences *themselves* he may have been), nor that he was unaware of the nefarious distraction of seeking such perfection instead of, say, fighting a famine. We could hazard a guess that Kierkegaard would not have wanted anybody to become preoccupied with being an exceptional benefactor instead of supporting an ethos in which ignoring a famine is automatically viewed as despicable. Having highlighted a distinction between the 'fruits' of love (which must always be real and may sometimes be visible) and 'consequences' (which may earnestly be sought but to no avail) in the context of Kierkegaard's 'Love's Hidden Life and Its Recognizability by Its Fruits' (WoL 5–16), Jamie Ferreira draws our attention to something significant in *Works of Love*:

> What is at stake in the resolute anticonsequentialism that Kierkegaard espouses is that loving works can be thwarted by nature or other people and may not come to observable fruition. [. . .] However, nothing in this discussion, which emphasizes the limited relevance of consequences or observable results, implies a cavalier attitude toward the concrete needs of other people. In fact, in this deliberation, Kierkegaard anticipates his later comments on love as an outward task when he condemns the thoughtlessness involved in 'thinking about [one's] own cares instead of thinking about the cares of the poor, perhaps seeking alleviation by giving to charity instead of wanting to alleviate poverty' (WoL 13–14). This simple distinction between 'fruits' and consequences (or achievements) will become important later in clarifying the criticism that in *Works of Love* Kierkegaard devalues this-worldly concrete needs [. . .].[14]

Nevertheless, with the idea of raising the level of our *common* starting assumptions about what is moral, and of improving a *climate* of responsibility for the neighbour we do seem to be venturing away from Kierkegaard. But perhaps we are thinking in a Kierkegaardian fashion in order to do so. If Kierkegaard were to object – as well he might – that really to be ethical is to allow others to rise to the challenge of being ethical in unfavourable conditions, without the help of a 'climate' (assuming he would have queried the idea of a 'climate', given his reservations about whatever is accomplished *en masse* – although this climate we envisage would not necessarily be *accomplished* as the work of a crowd, for all it may be so enjoyed) we could perhaps respond. For we could maintain that what is really ethical is to provide people with a sporting chance of having enough headroom to see how immense the demands of the ethical *always* are and then let us all individually rise to *that* challenge. And this structure, subjective and subjunctive, would be ongoing, open-ended and recursive in all the usual Kierkegaardian ways.

The crucial point is this: working for the creation of what we could call a 'climate of decency' is only an inevitable lightening of a person's ethical 'load' if you assume that there are set limits to the amount of ethical behaviour to be accomplished. But that is an assumption that Søren Kierkegaard, and some of the thinkers who came after him – like Emmanuel Levinas – seek to dismiss. Kierkegaard, as we acknowledged above, was profoundly suspicious of anything in the sphere of morals or religiousness being undertaken *en masse*. But here, again, is the answer that we could give to him: the creation of a climate of decency would not be undertaken by a multitude, even though its benefits may be enjoyed by a multitude. It could be undertaken by individuals who may think independently but still inspire one another, and by the 'time' its benefits are enjoyed, there is no need for anybody to carry on claiming or thinking that *this* is ethics; rather, this is just a climate. But that is not the end of the story, for although the climate may benefit a multitude, it is only a basis. A basis from which the members of the now better cared-for multitude can proceed to the next thing that ethics is going to be – *for the single individual.*

When looking at the future, which is very much the thing to do if we are considering what ethics means, now, for an individual, then for an action to pass as ethical in deontological terms a certain 'consequentialism' may be required, strange as it may seem. If, by contrast, a person consciously attempts to be ethical in a deontological way in the moment of acting, then to be sure, 'moral success' may be elusive in consequentialist terms (though that would perhaps be a contingent eventuality) but, ironically enough, the failure may be all the more spectacular in – precisely – deontological terms, because one has not had, as the unalloyed content of one's motivation, the concrete benefit of the other person, or people. One has not had the welfare of that other or those others immovably in one's sights. In Kierkegaardian terms, one has not had the 'one thing' of the other's good as the only thing. To bypass Kierkegaard's 'double-mindedness' (*Tvesindethed*) will be hard if one seeks the best for others *in addition* to willing that one's motivation be pure. (We know how suspicious Kierkegaard always was of anything being *in addition* to anything else!) Making it easier for others to behave well, on the basis of, say, a concern for the welfare of the more remote 'third man' – as Emmanuel Levinas might say – is a concrete goal that an ethical agent might do well deontologically to pursue, *and as if consequentialism were true* – as if, for example, consequentialism were not rendered categorically problematic by its assignation of values to motives on the basis of actual outcomes. All this could become more complicated, it must be admitted, if part of the good consequence for a particular neighbour is actually an apprehension of the deonotological or indeed consequentialist 'purity' of the giver's act. But this is not something which preoccupies Kierkegaard in a major way, with his firm emphasis on the giver's disappearance or at least upon his or her 'insignificance', and so it may not be appropriate to discuss such eventualities here.

vii. COMMUNITY AND INDIVIDUALITY

> [W]ith my new edifying discourses people will now probably scream out that I know nothing about what comes next, about sociality. The fools! (PJS 253)

Could there be a sense, then, in which Kierkegaard's activism on behalf of religious individuality, so far from inspiring a disdain for community, may rather prompt us to refresh or even reinvent an idea of what community – a word that has perhaps become rather foggy and flavourless in recent times – should mean? In connection with Kierkegaard the idea might seem surprising to some. However, an affirmative answer would not force us to skate over Kierkegaard's antipathy towards that 'crowd' whose supposed cowardice and sluggishness so many other thinkers (Schopenhauer, Nietzsche, Adorno) have deplored. Surely what Kierkegaard most vehemently decries is that subjectivity should *start* by attaching itself to a public 'they', and only think – if thinking is then the right word – afterwards. Surely the eventuality he most stridently warns against is that a person's subjectivity should actually be throttled by an amassed hodgepodge of received formulae and ready-made conclusions passing as observation or as analysis. Of course the avoidance of this sorry state of affairs can prove to be easier said than done, and not only for contingent historical reasons: if the aim is not to go round with a received formula and, as it were, play 'snap' with the world on one hand and the formula on the other, but rather, dispassionately to describe and assess entities and problems with reference to their unique attributes, this is probably going to be a relative rather than a radical improvement. For while a given entity's possession of an attribute might well single it out, the ascribing of the attribute still continues to involve a certain degree of 'snap'. We may think especially about attempts by historians and social commentators to pick out and describe this or that general malaise or putatively endemic phenomenon.

Now it may also be the case that Kierkegaard is unenthusiastic about *any* worldly alliance, and he may as a consequence be thought of as an extremist of sorts. But we, the students of Kierkegaard, are at liberty to suppose that if community is something we value (even if it is hard to establish precisely how it was valued by Kierkegaard), we may very well need a thoroughgoing account of individuality like Kierkegaard's, and we may need to second his endorsement of subjectivity and inwardness precisely in order to ensure that what we create truly deserves to be called a community. The concept of community depends upon that of individuality or, rather, upon that of numerous individualities (as opposed to what Kierkegaard most deplored: an individuality composed of a number). And sure enough, we have evidence in support of this from Kierkegaard:

> Not until the single individual has established an ethical stance despite the whole world, not until then can there be any question of genuinely uniting; otherwise it gets to be a union of people who separately are weak, a union as unbeautiful and depraved as a child-marriage. (TA 106)

Indeed, if community did not depend upon individuality, it would cancel itself out as a meaningful concept and simply amount to a placeholder for what was really just a bigger individuality, and not just in the Hegelian sense, as outlined, say, in *Philosophy of Right*, but rather in what Kierkegaard would think of as the Hegelian sense, which is a little bit different (in that it is a less accommodating, more 'levelling' and in fact less dialectical conception of 'bigger individuality' than what a sympathetic reader of Hegel would grant him). Perhaps this is why, in *The Present Age* ('Nytiden' is the title of a section in Kierkegaard's *En literair Anmeldelse* which inspired this choice of title for some English translations of what the Hongs brought out as *Two Ages*), Kierkegaard was careful not to mount tirades against *community*, saving them instead for that concept (that comprehensively doomed concept – at least as far as the works of Kierkegaard are concerned): 'the public' (*offentligheden*).

We could even gloss portions of Kierkegaard's invective against 'the public' as amounting to a complaint that 'the public' precisely does not signify 'community'. Indeed, one of the very attributes Kierkegaard is at pains to ascribe to 'the public' – while bemoaning, of course, the fact that it can be so ascribed – is, sure enough, *individuality*. The public acts like an individual. *This*, most assuredly, is not Kierkegaard's individual, his famous 'single individual'; far from it. The treatment by Kierkegaard of 'the public' in *The Present Age*, as if 'the public' referred to a single great animal of some kind is more than an entertaining rhetorical strategy. Kierkegaard really is arguing that the public's *individuality*, instantly arising and instantly disappearing as required, is just what is most grievous and what is most to be lamented. The public's individuality is monstrous not least because it is unaccountable. So when we hear it said that Kierkegaard spoke out for individuality we will concur, but it would be as well to observe that he did not wish to represent the cause of any or every 'individuality'. We have indicated that he had no truck with Hegelian individuality or at least his interpretation of it, for example. Presumably this is not because Hegelian individuality is faulty from an indicative point of view (indeed we may suppose that, judged indicatively, it is logically impeccable), but because from a subjunctive point of view it may militate against whatever mood is necessary for imagining that things can be taken in hand, or that the future can be 'changed' – that is, *shaped*. It is surely impossible, after all, to talk about changing the future, in the strict sense of the word 'change'. From what, exactly, would we be changing it? No, it makes more sense to speak of shaping the future.

Now to say that Kierkegaard hated the public is true. It is true as long as one understands that 'the public' – *that entity: 'the public'* – is what he hated and not, say: 'members of the public', unless of course the expression 'members of the public' were being used to designate the extent to which people are not belonging to themselves. To be sure, there are faint echoes, even in the non-pseudonymous works, of the Romantic depiction of the exceptional and extraordinary man, the lofty and unusual man (and, alas, it is indeed invariably a *man*), conceptions which often enough were elaborated at the expense of another conception – of supposedly ordinary people, but in the non-pseudonymous Kierkegaard there is never really the conscious celebration of arrogance and haughtiness that we might associate with Baudelaire, Nietzsche and with some of the protagonists of Stendhal or of Dostoevsky. This is not to say that Kierkegaard was never arrogant or haughty nor even that arrogance and haughtiness could never play a part in the life of a Kierkegaardian 'single individual'; Kierkegaard would presumably prefer such haughtiness to a cowering before the wisdom of 'the public' which – for all it is a cowering – manages also to be *pompous*. For what could be more infuriating than a *pompous cowering*? What could be more soul-destroying than an encounter with a consciousness that is condescendingly intransigent at the precise moment of surrendering to mediocrity? And what could be more dicey than a bid to try and *come to terms* with such wholesale adherence to the wisdom of 'the public' (as if democracy would be the sanctioning of a right to relinquish thought)? What could be worse than to come away from a dialogue, as Kierkegaard says, feeling that one has just been conversing with an anonymity (TA 103) (since one's interlocutor has spoken only the latest usages and not with an earnest or anxious voice, but only with the gossipy voice of 'the public')? Better, perhaps, for as many people as possible to be haughty, even if haughtiness may not seem very Christian, than to make any additions to all that hollowness. Yet in principle and in essence, Kierkegaard, who wanted to be a Christian, was not out to elevate any individual to the detriment of the rest nor to recommend haughtiness; he was committed to elevating the possibility of elevation for each and every individual. Kierkegaard's Anti-Climacus, for example, says simply that 'the single individual' is something 'which everyone can and should be' (PC 223).

The Dane may not have found it easy to commit the power of his thinking to the study of what community in this world ought to mean. Even admirers of both Kierkegaard and the ideal of community have conceded as much.[15] He feared that as soon as you have numbers acting in concert, there is a likelihood that responsibility will be diffused. His *Practice in Christianity* for example, contains many a stern reminder that when individuals are grouped, a dodging or passing-on of accountability (accountability, perhaps, for the injuries sustained by those outside the group) can become normal. But what if we were able to bring Kierkegaard's ideas, and especially that of the single individual and the dangers of 'levelling', into discussions of what words like 'community' and 'equality' might come to mean?

viii. DEMOCRACY AND EQUALITY

In the chapter of his *Kierkegaard* entitled 'Equality and Association', Alastair Hannay makes the suggestion, in the first of two divisions on the concept of 'levelling', that the key concern for Kierkegaard is not always a person's failure to act decisively through lack of courage, irresoluteness or fear of the personal consequences, but rather the extent to which, 'above any such qualms, [people] fear the "judgement of reflection"; they are afraid of reflection's indictment of them for venturing something *as individuals*.' This leads Hannay onto Hegel:

> This overriding respect for reflection's judgement is linked to the notion of association by an assumption of Hegelian philosophy [. . .]: namely that rationality, as the foundation of human action, growth, and freedom, is embodied in man's collective institutions. The fundamental principle is that such institutions are not obstacles to individual freedom, but its vehicles, even when the participants do not at first understand them as such—according to Hegel the state harmonizes the limited and more or less selfish interests of individual agents into a whole in which their separate interests are mutually served even before this fact is recognized.[16]

Hegel's account is not that controversial. And to a large degree we can see it borne out, or at least the expectation of its truth borne out, in the way that many western nation-states are organized today. However, with regard to societies in which this harmonization process takes the form of the democratic orchestration of services and regulation, it might be observed that it is not always made explicit what voters are being invited to do. Are they to express a preference for what they think will work best for them? Or are they to express a preference for what they think will work for all, or at least for the greatest number? Many commentators would quite understandably say that people will only ever vote for what is in their own best interest. This is entirely plausible, and indeed, it may actually desirable, since the majority of people can be expected to be *better informed* about what would be conducive to a better standard of living for themselves than about what would be conducive to improved conditions all round. And the most informed vote is presumably what serious democrats would value most (including those democrats who would like to hope that people's view of their own best interests would actually *include* a consideration for the needs of the society as a whole). It should be noted, though, that what we then have, at the end of an election, is not a representation of *a nation's view about the nation* but rather a demographic of a nation's personal interests (or wishes).

However, an interesting experiment for a democracy to conduct would be to stage an election whose ballot papers contained one invitation to vote according to what, by the voter's view, would best represent his or her material interests and another invitation to vote for what would, by the voter's view, best serve the collective material interest. Naturally, we might expect that many if not most of the ballot papers would contain the same vote for both invitations – although in many if not most cases such alignment would not necessarily be a sign of insincerity. If the outcome of such an election were based purely on the responses to the second invitation, the trust being invested in every voter would of course be considerable. If the outcome were based on the answers to both questions there would have to be apparatus in place to allow for two qualitatively distinct forms of representation in a parliament. Each party would receive a pair of results. Wherever there was a divergence in the votes registered (or seats counted) for a party according to how it was perceived as an advocate of personal economic interest, on one hand, and, on the other hand, as an advocate of the economic interests of society as a whole – we would have certainly have an interesting result.

Of course, in real life it is hard enough to be sure that voters are sufficiently informed about their own best interests, let alone the interests of the collective, impartially viewed, for any given election to be considered a tribute to the ideals of democracy. But the key point as far as Kierkegaard is concerned is this: if there were an opportunity to vote according to a view about the interests of society as a whole, that very opportunity might stimulate a willingness to become better informed about the needs of the neighbour. Moreover, if people were explicitly invited to register their opinion on that subject (perhaps there are some who already use their votes to do this) they would be participating in a process that would embody at least one major principle of Kierkegaard's conception of neighbour-love: that it is not to be preferential. Alastair Hannay picks up on this:

> We saw that for Kierkegaard the content of the moral (and therefore unified) will is unselfish concern for others. This concern is already an exercise of sociality in the broad sense of that term. But it might also be claimed to be an exercise of sociality in a more precise sense: in so far as the unselfishness of the concern immunizes it from partiality, it might reasonably be said to be itself an actual embodiment of social harmony.[17]

There is another Kierkegaardian dimension to what might seem like a hopelessly high-minded notion of a separate vote that is explicitly to relate to an opinion about the general good. It might well bring out the single individual. This may seem strange to say, given that the voter is being invited to put his or her individual needs not entirely aside but on a level – yes, a level – with those of the neighbour. But we should bear in mind that Kierkegaard's much-talked-about individualism is most assuredly not an economic individualism. And not only would the voting individual, when responding to (let us call it) 'the second invitation' not be *levelled* by the activism of the party that he or she has chosen for (let us call it) 'the first invitation' – albeit activism on behalf of his or her economic best interests – but, more importantly, this individual would escape from the *levelling* of economic self-interest as such. For the idea that each person has a responsibility (Kierkegaard would surely smile at this) – *a civic duty*, no less – to register an opinion about his or her own material interest could certainly fit among the levelling forces that preoccupy Kierkegaard. The 'civic duty' idea that we do have in currency is, to be fair, something of a hint that we should at least try to think of our neighbours when we vote, but Kierkegaard would probably think that there was something comic in the pleasant and cosy solemnity of us all becoming pillars of society when we set off for the polling station 'ready to do our bit' – *for ourselves*, and for others to a degree – although not to a ridiculous degree. But for ourselves – definitely. And after all, a good sensible mixture of selfishness and unselfishness is perfectly respectable, and in a way, almost Christian.

But to be serious again, a vote that was explicitly focused on the welfare of the neighbour might well spring us out of the levelling that surely does guarantee equality even ahead of an election: the assumption that we must all be looking out for ourselves. To be free of *that* equality, albeit for a moment – when answering 'the second invitation' – might throw up a chance of better equality of the sort that makes a difference to the neighbour. Even if enhanced quality of life for our neighbours does not guarantee them access to what Kierkegaard thinks of as the highest, it might help them to be housed, to be educated, to be cared for in old age, and when sick – and all these things are not necessarily a bad basis from which to seek the grace of the Lord, even if Kierkegaard would be quick to urge that the grace of the Lord is precisely what is there for the poor soul who lacks all these things, is the wealth that no lack of these things can take from him or her. Besides, the altruistic voter would, as we have suggested, be breaking away from the generality of self-interest, in the thick of which it surely is hard to become a single individual in the strictly Kierkegaardian sense. Self-interest, after all, is certainly held in common.

ix. ADORNO'S CRITIQUE

Theodor W. Adorno is known to have been highly critical of Kierkegaard. But it is perhaps to Adorno (as one who definitely was engaged very extensively with the economic and the social dimensions of human life) that we can turn if we want to see what it is about Kierkegaard that might be most problematic for those wanting to recover elements of his outlook for use in future models of community while seeking, as it were, that 'alternative ending' of which we have made mention. Quoting from the second part of *Either/Or*, Adorno writes as follows:

> Wherever the 'moralist' happens to speak of those conflicts that can occur between inwardness (represented by marriage) and the material situation (poverty), he justifies inwardness with the cozy cynicism of the petty-bourgeois *rentier*: 'When, for example poverty is proposed as a difficulty with which marriage may have to contend, I would answer: "Work—then all obstacles give way." Since we are now relying on our imaginations, you will perhaps take advantage of your poetic licence and make answer: "They couldn't get any work. The decline in business and in the shipping trade has left a great many people without bread." Or you permit them to get a little work, but it is not sufficient. In my opinion, by wise economy they surely could have been able to make both ends meet.' The logic of the argument bears witness against itself. And still it goes too far for Kierkegaard. While he recognizes the

> influence of business cycles on the possibility of savings, he extracts the entire crisis as an 'arbitrary invention of poetic licence' from a period in which, at the same time that *Either/Or* was being written, the most terrible impoverishment of the English industrial proletariat was taking place.[18]

Adorno, it must be said, is not especially keen to take seriously the distinctions between the pseudonyms, and something that a Kierkegaard scholar might, when searching for the limitations of a particular life-view being *critiqued* by Kierkegaard, perceive as a dead give-away, will appear in Adorno's account as merely an aspect of Kierkegaard's mentality. Perhaps the harshness of the mentality depicted by Adorno's choice of extracts above is a case in point. However, if it is indeed Kierkegaard's own harshness we are meant to be seeing here, then perhaps Adorno nevertheless underestimates the degree to which much of this Kierkegaaardian harshness is fundamentally self-directed, the harshness of a son standing in 'against' himself on behalf of an absent father. For all Adorno's emphasis on what he terms the 'immanent dialectic' that was indeed so fundamental to Kierkegaard, there may be insufficient recognition in *Construction of the Aesthetic* (*Konstruktion des Ästhetischen*) of the ongoing conversation Kierkegaard was having with himself through the medium of the authorship. To observe that 'dialogue' in motion, we can look especially at the signed works including texts like 'The Gospel of Sufferings' (UDVS 213–341) and the two discourses on patience from 1844.[19] Problems can arise when Kierkegaard tries to benefit his reader by exporting the art of self-directed harshness; a callous, or at least ignorant, disregard for the material necessities of others can seem to lie behind the proffered edification.

What lies behind the texts for Adorno, though, is what he takes to be a dysfunctional understanding of freedom. Having correctly summarized Kierkegaard's presentation of equality as that which can only truly be produced among neighbours before God, Adorno seems to carry out the analysis as if Kierkegaard is misguidedly expecting the freedom of inwardness – that does indeed embrace the neighbour in, say, *Works of Love* – to be presupposed (but presumably now as a different sort of freedom) in the external world; a world that only *exists* for Kierkegaard to the extent that it does not disappoint that expectation. To the extent that it does disappoint, Adorno thinks, Kierkegaard's philosophy will simply recoil and flee. On the concept of equality, Adorno may be rejecting outright any distinction whatsoever between the inward equality, on one hand, of the Kierkegaardian eternal and, on the other hand, of that which pertains to socio-economic relations. Or he may be only rejecting suggestions that the former is bound up with the latter. Either way, he is not optimistic about Kierkegaard's proposals:

> This equality is not achieved when human relations are so preformed by the domination of exchange-value, the division and commodity form of labour, that one 'neighbour' can no more respond spontaneously to the other for more than an instant than the individual's kindness suffices to do him any good, let alone have an effect on the social structure. Thus Kierkegaard's ethics is contentless.—This ethics originates in his concept of freedom. Such a concept does not remain, as does the Kantian concept, in the realm of the intelligible, surrendering the empirical realm to necessity. It establishes itself in the empirical, and the empirical world is tolerated only insofar as it is the arena of freedom. Society contracts to the circumference of free 'neighbours,' while precisely its necessities are shunted aside as 'accidental' from the gates of philosophy. Freedom determines the self, which Kierkegaard conceives exclusively in its freedom, just as it determines society. If the material necessities of society are denied in the name of freedom, the necessities and the reality of the instincts vanish from the self according to the same scheme. Kierkegaard's absolute self is mere spirit. The individual is not the sensuously developed person, and no property is accorded him beyond the bare necessities. Inwardness does not consist in its fullness but is ruled over by an ascetic spiritualism.[20]

But while much of this critique would be entirely germane to an understanding of the all-important and fundamental difference between Adorno and existentialism as such, it may remain open to debate whether or not Kierkegaard's freedom – to the extent that its meaning ever exceeds that of a galvanizing rhetoric – *does* differ from that of Kant, of whom it is indeed reasonable to say that his freedom stays 'in the realm of the intelligible, surrendering the empirical realm to necessity.' If Kierkegaard's freedom 'establishes itself in the empirical' this may only be true in the sense that his dialectic aims to equip subjectivity with more than one way of reacting to the inevitable and the definitive, and not that peasants must take responsibility for failing to move mountains. If Adorno were to reply that such ways-of-reacting amount in Kierkegaard to what he (Adorno) calls the *indifferentiation of subject and object*, then it is perhaps Adorno himself who, albeit as a consequence of getting in close to his subject, is giving ground to the experimental suppositions of (especially Fichtean) romantic idealism.

Nevertheless, Adorno is not wrong to stress the pursuit of the indifferentiation of subject and object in Kierkegaard. An extract from a letter to his sister-in-law Henriette Kierkegaard is enough to show this:

> Often in my childhood I was not permitted by my father to walk to Frederiksberg, but I walked hand in hand with him up and down the floor—to Frederiksberg. (LD 174)

That dash tells you half the story. The sudden statement after it – 'to Frederiksberg' – tells you everything. It might be defiance towards a world – an outside world – that the world as conjured rather than as encountered is taken as the ultimate reality. Or it might be that Kierkegaard's love for the father is what will govern which Frederikesberg is to be the real one, thus indicating, perhaps, that the only reality at the bottom of Kierkegaard's world is love.

It would be strange, then, if Kierkegaard's freedom were really seeking to establish itself in a world beyond, as appears to be suggested in that earlier quotation. And in a way, Adorno is already accepting this, precisely by limiting *Kierkegaard's* 'world' to an interior:

> On the offensive, his philosophy responds to the painful intrusion of reality into the objectless interior, marked by recessive movement of the self. This accounts for Kierkegaard's political opinions. However consistently they fail to grasp the circumstances, they are more deeply formed by them than the blatantly reactionary, provincial, and individualistic thesis (particularly in the *Diaries*) would ever lead one to imagine.[21]

Adorno, despite the vehemence of his critique, is arguably showing lenience to Kierkegaard's philosophy in some respects when he takes the Dane's political pronouncements as mere symptoms of a retreat, to be understood, perhaps, as a psychological issue, from all objects. (His portrayal of Kierkegaard's cultural narrow-mindedness may indeed, to be fair, count as a different matter.) We may also want to query the idea that the characteristics under discussion are mainly exhibited when the philosophy is 'on the offensive'; it could be that Kierkegaard *really* going 'on the offensive' is exactly what will break him out from all the vulnerabilities, neurotic and otherwise, which menace that circle of objectless immanence – if there is one – to which Adorno is so attentive.

An 'alternative ending' may really be what we are seeking, because if Kierkegaard is to be 'rescued' – not conscripted into the service of any particular politics, but 'rescued' as having *any* relevance to the existence of a political sphere as such – we will find ourselves with a struggle on our hands if we try to argue this on the basis that since Kierkegaard's philosophy contains humanistic principles then he must already in some sense be doing politics. His exact words were 'I hate politics' (M 60) – and in this case we should perhaps not dismiss Kierkegaard's talk as a mere symptom of the retreat from the world and from all history that Adorno apprehends; it is closer to an actual ingredient of that retreat. The light-headed, pretentious conservativism of Kierkegaard's early polemical experiments or the reactionary outbursts in the journals may, as mere symptoms of something psychologically deeper, be *in themselves* shallow and less than coherent; it is true that they may not be relatable in any interesting way to the real philosophy of Kierkegaard. But 'I hate politics' – though it could be taken as itself an ideological remark – probably gets closer to the real content of the philosophical outlook as well as being a part of the real retreat from objectivity (from 'objectivity' in the general sense and in the sense understood by dialectical materialism). Interestingly enough, the remark, *in Kierkegaard's case and as regards his philosophy* may not be a sign of conservatism that is masked or merely latent. However, this is not to deny that he may – *in addition* – have been a conservative of sorts.

With his 'I hate politics' it looks as if Kierkegaard is *not* imagining that the political could provide a suitable arena for the manifestation of love for the neighbour. It is hard to avoid this inference, and that is why the 'alternative ending' probably has to be ours not his. The 'alternative ending' in which Kierkegaard's thought will be of service to constructive ideas about economics and the social can be *based on* what he says; this much has been meticulously demonstrated by Leo Stan, Jamie Ferreira, Alastair Hannay and several others. But perhaps it cannot easily be *construed within* what he says.

As for Kierkegaard's apparently chilly indifference towards the social problems that can supposedly remedied by just working even harder, there is perhaps one way we can to a degree redeem the Dane. We would do this by concentrating on the fact of there being two wholly different worlds – two different dimensions even – appearing in Kierkegaard, one of which appears very seldom. These two wholly different worlds are represented by the third person or 'objective' view on one hand, and, on the other hand, the position of *subjectivity as directly addressed*. The first and second person conjugations are the only ones that exist in this world. Subjectivity may be addressed by itself, by another, by itself in place of another (Søren addressed by himself in lieu of his father Michael Pedersen), or by another in place of itself (the 'single reader' addressed by 'the discourse' intended ultimately to stand in for conscience). We always have to remember that with Kierkegaard this latter world, the world of the direct address, is by far the favoured one. If Kierkegaard had consistently shown signs of being seriously concerned with the former, it surely would be hard to rescue him for the political or the social. It is the very fact that he only ever wants to talk to *you*, and specifically about how *you* could start talking to *yourself* that makes the key difference. And sometimes, the hope that *this* is the essential axis of communication is actually underlined by Kierkegaard with precisely a movement away to something that is *different again* from that axis:

> *You* shall, *you* shall love the neighbour. O my listener, it is not *you* to whom *I* am speaking; it is *I* to whom eternity says: *You* shall. (WoL 90)

This does bear out the idea that at the heart of Kierkegaard what we have is the subjectivity that gives itself a 'talking-to' – perhaps in the way a father would his child. The key issue in Kierkegaard is that *I* as *I* – let us not even say 'me', since the use of even this object pronoun might lead us away from the spirit of the thing – *can always act. I* as *I* – can always *act upon myself* (even if I cannot chop down a mountain). This 'can' is not really anything that can be regarded as denoting a state of affairs, an already existing fact; rather, as said by a person to himself or to herself, this 'can' is fundamentally subjunctive in character. More specifically, it is *highly subjunctive*, which is to say that the subjunctivity in question is not an epistemic subjunctivity that could imminently or eventually be 'settled' with the walling up of some gap or other in the totality of propositional knowledge. No, because even if you *did in fact* 'pull yourself together' or 'dig yourself out of that hole' or 'triumph in adversity' or 'finally get a grip' – none of these successes would amount to clear evidence that 'I can' had been true at the time. They do not show that your claim turned out to be true. They may well suggest to you that you *did well* to say to yourself: 'I *can*!' But are they proof that this 'claim' referred accurately – or for that matter inaccurately – to anything at all that *was* the case? The answer is yes if 'I *can*' was from a sentence like 'I *can* join you on Thursday because the other appointment has now been postponed' – 'I can' in the sense of 'I am at liberty to . . .' and so on. But the 'I *can*' of getting-a-grip, taking the initiative and the like, is harder to trace as true or false. However, if the sentence played a part in the recovery or the getting-of-a-grip, then despite the grammatically indicative status of the utterance, the position has been subjunctive (as a relating to what only *might* be so), and highly subjunctive (in that the substantive content following this *might* will not be conclusively shown by either success or failure).

This may be the only way to rescue existentialism as a whole, indeed, or at least a way to rescue a starting place for the whole of existentialism; rescuing the whole of it may be another matter. But while the 'I *as* I' approach can work well, can be efficient – so *very* – efficient in *this* world (with everything that Kierkegaard intends when he mentions *this world*; who knows how it may stand in any other?) it may be inhumane to submit this 'can' – this 'Work!' – as a potential policy for a town or for a nation or for the population of a continent or even for any human being other than oneself.

Kierkegaard's pronouncements will appear unreasonable and unfeeling, *unless* it is not in any sense a potential decree or a potential policy; not even a general report on what is needful (as all political theory must inevitably be), but rather an *address*. The idea would be that Kierkegaard's thoughts are not at all indicative, but instead are his commended ways for a person to talk to himself or herself (just as the prayers with which many of the discourses begin are offered as ways for a person to talk to God). But if there is to be an 'alternative ending' then Kierkegaard's commendation of the

'I *as* I' approach ought not to equate with complete dismissal of society viewed 'objectively' as Kierkegaard would say; far from it. Circulation of what should correctly be seen as *an existentialism* in him (here he is by no means the mere uncle or godfather of that movement but rather its unambiguous founder) becomes an ethical issue, an ethical issue that should lead us – just as it perhaps ought to have led Kierkegaard – into the political and social spheres, and not to statements like 'I hate politics'.

He may have hated politics, but some commentators will countenance the possibility that it was precisely a political change in Denmark that enabled Kierkegaard to publish, with relative impunity, the article criticizing Hans Lassen Martensen's eulogy of Bishop Mynster, an article that constituted the opening salvo of his whole attack on the Danish Church, but an article he had held back for some time, even after Martensen's appointment to the Episcopal See left vacant by the death of Mynster. Having noted that Martensen's appointment had been supported by an 'extremely conservative' Prime Minister, one A. S. Ørsted, Josiah Thompson observes that Kierkegaard had accepted in his journal the prospect of having to pay court costs arising from the reaction that his article was likely to produce. Nevertheless, Kierkegaard sat on the article through most of 1854. In his mind he was defiant. However, Thompson reasons as follows:

> But he must also have been aware of Section 8 of the *Law of the Use of the Press of January 3, 1851*, which carried a one- to six-month jail sentence for anyone who in print ridiculed the established religious teaching and/or practice. With Ørsted simultaneously holding the posts of Prime Minister and Cultus Minister, Kierkegaard could count on swift prosecution under this law. But on December 12, 1854, Ørsted's government fell, to be replaced by a liberal regime under P. G. Bang as Prime Minister and C. C. Hall as Cultus Minister. Six days later, on December 18, 1854, Kierkegaard published his reply to Martensen in *Fatherland*.[22]

Moreover, with this article and with the fiery one-man campaign it heralded, first in the paper *Fatherland* (*Fædreland*) and then in his own pamphlet *The Moment* (*Øieblikket*), Kierkegaard *was* – for better or for worse – leaving his *interior* and stepping forward into a social sphere. It may be significant that Adorno displays a certain respect for Kierkegaard's output in this final phase of the authorship. More than that, he – Adorno of all people – detects in these writings of Kierkegaard the beginnings of a radicalized consciousness[23] (thus complementing rather than contradicting the efforts of thinkers like M. Jamie Ferreira and Hugh Pyper[24] who discover the social in Kierkegaard in his ethical injunctions and Biblical inspirations):

> Kierkegaard gladly played off left-Hegelian materialist authors, such as Boerne and Feuerbach, against an empty idealist philosophy of identity—against a church he thought less knowledgeable of the essence of Christianity than precisely Feuerbach; behind his ironic-dialectical intention, a secret affinity may be hidden. There is enough materialist explosive present in the *Instant*, and the either/or of inwardness must, once shaken by the impact of the subsistent, reverse into its antithesis as Kierkegaard asserts the thesis. The efficient cause, however, hidden in the 'subsistent,' which the 'situation' reveals, is none other than knowledge of the reification of social life, the alienation of the individual from a world that comes into focus as mere commodity.[25]

At any rate, this was a move into *the world*, a move away from ambiguity, possibility and the inwardness (with all its marvellous freedoms) that Adorno has branded 'objectless', a move towards the indicative and a setting aside of subjunctive 'categories' and dreams. Perhaps with Kierkegaard's much narrower accommodation – he was then living in a small flat in Klædeboderne – his consciousness was not as 'roomy' as he had once complained it had been,[26] and perhaps there simply was not as much space for all that *objectless inwardness*. But perhaps this was ultimately to him *no matter*. And however ill-advised or misguided it may have been in some respects, for Kierkegaard himself this campaign was even, perhaps, the very thing he had so often felt was missing from his existence (and perhaps not delivered to him by such a multi-voiced artistic production – signed works included), a thing we discussed earlier in connection with the real meaning of ethics: *sheer action*.

x. KIERKEGAARD ON THE OFFENSIVE

Bishop Mynster died in the January of 1854. Mynster had been a friend to the Kierkegaard family. He had confirmed the young Søren in 1828, had officiated at the many Kierkegaard family funerals and had written sermons that Søren would read to his father and also to Regine. The style of Kierkegaard's own edifying discourses is considered to have been much influenced by them. In the early 1850s Kierkegaard's disenchantment with established Christianity was growing, but he did not want there to be open combat between himself and Mynster, whom he visited regularly through this time. For Kierkegaard, this was partly a matter of not offending against his own father's memory; the launching of a full-frontal attack while Mynster was alive did not strike him as acceptable or appropriate. With Mynster now departed, Kierkegaard felt the situation was different, and the prompt for his decision to go on the offensive was something in Martensen's eulogy:

> What fired Kierkegaard's anger was Martensen's use of the term 'witness to the truth' (*Sandhedsvidne*), which at that time could be found in no Danish dictionary for the simple reason that it was a recent Kierkegaard coinage. Kierkegaard had used it to characterize those martyrs and apostles who, in their suffering, 'witnessed' the truth of Christianity.[27]

This marked the beginning of the final phase of Kierkegaard's activity as writer and – insomuch as his polemics were in full swing right up until he collapsed in the street – the final phase of his life. Nevertheless, he did, as we have mentioned, wait a few months before publishing that first response to the eulogy. These articles are gathered together in the Hongs' edition as '*The Moment' and Late Writings*. They are variously considered to be compelling, trenchant, shrill, mordant, repetitious, funny, withering, lively, salutary and futile. Martensen himself only responded to the first; Kierkegaard interpreted the silence of the clergy after that as a further indictment of that whole section of Danish society.

There can be no denying that Kierkegaard's polemics do zip along and of course, as pieces of 'journalism' – of a sort – they do constitute evidence of his versatility as writer. Moreover, the campaign provided Kierkegaard with that much longed-for *idea* upon which he could stake himself; we might even go so far as to say it was a *telos* about which he could be *passionate*. Most interesting to us at this point perhaps is that the campaign did project him into direct engagement with social affairs, even if for him it was – to the best of his knowledge – all about

Christianity. And we would not want to begrudge Kierkegaard the oddly revivifying effect that the whole affair appears to have had upon him, to judge by the accounts of chance meetings with Hans Brøchner and indeed Regine Olsen.[28] But if we can just step back from admiration (or otherwise) for Kierkegaard the stylist, and from a follower's natural pleasure at the thought of an artist's energies revived – though Kierkegaard himself would note how the predicament of the consumptive is often at its most grave just when the patient feels best – and ask about the *content*. What about the main thrust of this energetic and reasonably extended phase of Kierkegaard's work? What do we make of this campaign's *raison d'être*?

In the preface to his biography of Kierkegaard, Josiah Thompson says what, in all fairness, has been said in various ways by many others, something that has no doubt been announced in hundreds of lectures to thousands of students, that Kierkegaard 'exposed the mendacity of conventional "lip-service" Christianity'.[29] But did he really *expose* the 'mendacity' or did he just *say that* it was going on? What, specifically, did he *expose*? That the pastors and bishops were not being sufficiently reviled, persecuted and – to mention one of his most oft-used examples – *spat upon*, in order to be able to claim that they were – what? – true Christians? Or *witnesses to the truth*? (And how consistent, anyway, was Kierkegaard in upholding the clarity of this distinction?) Well, either way, if they do not even count as Christians in his eyes, then it looks as if Kierkegaard may have put aside Johannes de Silentio's insight about, precisely, his *lack* of insight as evinced when he imagines himself reacting to a meeting with a knight of faith: 'Good Lord, is this the man, is this really the one – he looks just like a tax collector!' (FT/R 39). And if this be deemed an unsatisfactory protest on the grounds that Silentio is only a pseudonym, then let us just ask: whatever happened to *love hiding a multitude of sins*? Whatever happened to presupposing love on the part of the other, despite seeming evidence to the contrary? Whatever happened, in short, to 'judg[ing] not, lest [we] be judged'? Has Kierkegaard forgotten everything? Has he forgotten all the discourses and 'deliberations' which did not, on the whole, sanctimoniously admonish anyone, but which were used by Kierkegaard, we could reasonably wager, as ways to teach himself?

More specific to this particular battle against the established church, is it really not a terribly awkward shift in Kierkegaard's view of the world, given that for so long he scrupulously observed the distinction between his own status as a kind of lay-preacher of the written word and the status of ordained ministers who possess 'authority'? And it cannot be reliably or even very convincingly maintained that all his references in the 1840s to his being 'without authority' were meaningfully ironic (apart from having just a little bit of light irony from time-to-time; but this looks more like irony at the expense of his own rather odd predicament than any serious mockery of the clergy).

Even if there were one or two – or, for that matter, quite a few – double-minded self-servers among the Danish clergy of the 1850s, would not even the strictest New Testament Christianity have allowed Kierkegaard to have prayed for those individuals and to have reflected the concerns of those prayers in actions less abrasive and potentially more efficacious than those actions undertaken in *The Moment*? It may not be unchristian to be afraid that your neighbour has gone astray. Surely, however, the lesson offered in *Works of Love* and *Eighteen Upbuilding Discourses* is that it *would* be unchristian to stop hoping that those who have drifted away from goodness cannot be brought back or bring themselves back. Now that lesson, gentle and kind though at first it may appear, in fact places a colossally tough requirement upon all those seeking to follow the Christian teaching. Moreover, in some cases it may be colossally *inadvisable*. (And yes, even in Kierkegaard's brighter years, Johannes Climacus does warn us that what is Christian will often, if not inevitably, clash with what is prudent.) But that is the New Testament lesson, whether we like it or not, and was not that *Kierkegaard's* lesson *whether he liked it or not*?

It is not that well-meaning people everywhere can never have grounds for becoming periodically (or even perpetually – though this is perhaps not to be recommended from a health point of view[30]) enraged at the hypocrisy of a politician or perhaps the mealy-mouthed duplicity of a high-ranking civil servant, captain of industry or, for that matter, of an archbishop. But Kierkegaard had made it his business[31] in the 1840s to spread the Gospel and, inspired by Luke, Paul, Peter and James, to endorse and espouse the virtue of charity and specifically of *charitable ways of perceiving*. He had undertaken this at length and with great care and his 'findings' – so to speak – would not look at all out of place alongside – and at various points would be entirely consonant with – the philosophies of the great twentieth century advocates of *difficult kindness* like Simone Weil and Emmanuel Levinas. Why, then, did Kierkegaard become so unremittingly antagonistic towards the Church and, let us be clear, towards *the people* of the Church? Why so unyielding and undialectical? Whatever happened to the *communication of capability* which, contrary to implications by certain commentators, need not be inextricably wedded to the principles of 'indirect communication' (principles which, in all fairness, he may have had perfectly sound strategic *and* honourable reasons to abandon in the later years)?

Does not being beaten and bashed, though it may be grounds for Christians to give thanks, albeit dialectically,[32] for not having had their faith tested in this way, *prove* that they are only paying 'lip service'? What, precisely did Kierkegaard *expose*? Kierkegaard reproaches those clergy occupying positions whose trappings do signify opulence. But unfortunately his diatribes are stymied by a simultaneous bemoaning of the fact that priests are paid at all. He thereby deprives himself of a clear angle from which he could have defined himself as offering a corrective to what may indeed have been a slipping away from the true values of the New Testament. What incentive would there have been for anyone who *was* perhaps a less-than-wholly-self-examining pastor to set aside those luxuries which produce an infelicitous difference from the example set by Jesus, if Kierkegaard is also implying that all pastors, just because they are paid, must therefore only be in it for the money? If that is his view, then why even bother to mention the silk and the velvet? And did Kierkegaard not think for a moment that it might be acceptable *even in the eyes of the eternal* that pastors should provide – yes – a *service*? Could he not have accepted, as he seems to have been able to do in the 1840s[33] that a pastor making *a good job* of, say, a funeral service, could be quite important for the one who is bereaved? Unfortunately we cannot really take the heat off Kierkegaard by referring to his claims that he would have no objection if only pastors would all accept that they were just merchants. These cannot be taken seriously; the whole idea smacks of sarcasm.

Kierkegaard's communications perhaps had a better chance of success[34] in the days when, as a slightly younger (and, yes, considerably richer) man, he produced that impressively subtle and dialectical question 'How much, then, is the little that a person needs?' (EUD 297) – a question which, for all that, is arguably no less fundamentally demanding than anything he said in the *Fatherland* articles or in *The Moment*. It is a question in the third person, yes, but what a great *communication of capability*! The discourse can be observed or overheard asking that question *about a person*, or just of itself, perhaps – but in reality: what a thoroughly pointed collaring of me, the reader, what a button-holing of you, the reader, what a profound hesitation about himself, the author of, in this case, 'To Need God Is a Human Being's Highest Perfection'! The question is dialectical by being able to persist in opposition to any actual answer. It is the question of self-examination even though the words are simply: *How much, then, is the little that a person needs?*

The 'much' is the part of the question that comes from earth – and who would deny that it is *only reasonable* to think about the issue of how much? But the 'little' – where does this 'little' come from? It comes from the acceptance that yes, when all is said and done, it may be that in contrast to what we assume we need, a little is enough. And now please can we move on? But no! The question will not *quite* let us move on! Because, not unreasonably – if we do concede that a little is, on reflection, probably enough – the question still stands and wants to check with us: *how much is that little*? Heavens, we all have busy lives and we may (quite understandably) have hoped that by granting this point about *the little* there would not then be a further question about *the much* – the *much* that might still be stored inside *the little*! Of course these terms are relative, but the question already unashamedly announces its knowledge of that! The question will not make itself indicative by proposing what could be an agreed plan for repayment of the much. Far be it from the question to inconvenience us by taking up that much space on the paper. But by taking up not very much space on the paper, there is a possibility that it will take up quite a bit of space in the mind of the one Kierkegaard calls *his reader*.[35]

Who is Kierkegaard's reader? By that, we mean: who is the one Kierkegaard calls *his* reader? It is completely true that every one of us is his intended reader – hence the personal tone of the reading material! And who *was* his intended reader? Well, we think it was most especially the one who was once his intended: his beloved Regine. We will come back to Regine Olsen in just a moment. But first we must sum up on the matter of how we have started with Kierkegaard.

xi. ALTERNATIVE ENDINGS

What have we learned? That Kierkegaard only has relevance to conversations about 'community' if we change what he said? No, not necessarily, but perhaps we have seen that there were conversations about the social that Kierkegaard only started, conversations that we might do well to see as yet to be completed. If we care about the social then starting with Kierkegaard might just prove to be a rather good idea. But he might not be able to take us to the end of anything or even as far as the middle. If the ending he does offer lies in the world of spirit, then yes, let that be a matter for each and every individual. But for living in this world, insomuch and for as long as we have to do so, it could be that an alternative or complementary ending is required. And would Kierkegaard be enraged or appalled at the suggestion? Not necessarily, for despite all his fears about the having of two minds – and his fear, indeed, that even to have a mind at all is in some sense to be perpetually divided – there is a sense in which the double-sidedness he encountered in all thinking served him well. Moreover, he was capable of believing – not in defiance of but *in addition to* what was actually the case – in the almost concrete importance of a certain possible world persisting as an alternative right alongside the one we have. His own alternative ending is to be found in one final 'as if' and the curious *reality* of this last 'as if' will perhaps resonate most freely if, having only started with Kierkegaard, we nevertheless give him the final word:

Document XXI. *Will*

Dear Brother,

It is, of course, my will that my former fiancée, Mrs. Regine Schlegel, inherit without condition whatever little I may leave. If she herself will not accept it, she is to be asked if she would be willing to administer it for distribution to the poor.

What I wish to give expression to is that to me an engagement was and is just as binding as a marriage, and that therefore my estate is her due, exactly as if I had been married to her.

Your brother
S. Kierkegaard

[*Address*:]
To Dr. Kierkegaard, pastor.
To be opened after my death. (DL xxv–xxvi and 33)

NOTES

CHAPTER 1: INTRODUCTION, HISTORICAL CONTEXT AND BIOGRAPHICAL OUTLINE

1. George Pattison, *'Poor Paris!' – Kierkegaard's Critique of the Spectacular City* (Berlin, 1999), p. 17.
2. Niels Thulstrup, though, finds against the Dane on this: 'Kierkegaard mentions [Hegel's 'attempt to begin with nothing'] as a phenomenon typical of the age; but neither he himself nor any of the scholars who have commented on his first book have noted the discrepancy with Hegel himself. Kierkegaard obviously has read neither *Phenomenology of the Spirit* nor *Lectures on the History of Philosophy*, which Michelet edited beginning in 1833; but – as his note on the next page shows – he has obviously seen the table of contents of Hegel's *Science of Logic*. Had Kierkegaard only read Hegel's prefaces to the first and second editions of that work and the introductory section "With what must the science begin," he would hardly have written what he did here. For Hegel, logic begins chiefly with "being" [. . .]. What Kierkegaard has written is simply incorrect; in Hegel pure "being" turns out to be identical with pure "nothing," but it is not immediately understood in that way.' *Kierkegaard's Relation to Hegel* (Princeton, 1980), p. 168. However, Thulstrup deals here with the period September 1838 to July 1840, and specifically with *From the Papers of One Still Living* (*Af en endnu Levendes Papirer*). Kierkegaard was better acquainted with Hegel's work by the time of the *Postscript*, and by the mid-1840s he usually refers only to *philosophy's* attempt to start with nothing. The target of the jokes about starting with nothing in *Johannes Climacus* might as well be Descartes, as anybody else, and the laborious divisions of the narrative into paragraphs with convoluted headings could be as much a satire on Kant as on Hegel.
3. 'Sin for Hegel [. . .] is but a "negative" which can be "annulled"; and faith is but a "first immediacy", resting, that is upon immediate, embryonic, intimate feelings which make a man grope after – something. Its vagueness, says Hegel, must be superseded by knowledge, and this

by the exercise of the intellect, which will lead a man to Truth, albeit by a different path than religion. The goal is the same, however. Religion and Speculative Philosophy have the same content but a different form. S.K. disagrees fundamentally. Sin cannot be merely "annulled" by thought. And faith in its fulness is a "second immediacy", not a first; i.e. an inner feeling – which comes after acknowledging sin, and after "Repetition" and the "new birth".' 'Assessment', T. H. Croxall's introduction to his translation of *Johannes Climacus or De Omnibus Dubitandum Est* (Stanford, 1967), p. 43.

4. *Phenomenology of Spirit*, translated by A. V. Miller (Oxford, 1977), p. 375.
5. *Crisis in the Life of an Actress and Other Essays on Drama*, translated with an introduction by Stephen D. Crites (New York, 1967), p. 27.
6. Kierkegaard's caution against the idea that '[w]e are all Christians' on the basis of being inhabitants of Christendom was to be central element in *The Moment* (*Øieblikket*) – also translated as *The Instant*. The view that Christendom had parted company with real Christianity was upheld on his behalf right at the very end, when his nephew Henrik Sigvard Lund made an unauthorized speech at the burial.
7. Transcripts of the addresses given by Peter Christian Kierkegaard at the two Roskilde conventions make up Appendix B of *Encounters with Kierkegaard: A Life as Seen by His Contemporaries*, collected, edited and annotated by Bruce H. Kirmmse and translated with Virginia R. Laursen (Princeton, 1996), pp. 256–268.
8. 'Apropos of this: Do you know the following anecdote? A.: "Well, Kierkegaard, now you can get out of studying for your examinations because you no longer have your father urging you all the time." K.: "No. Don't you see my friend, that now I can no longer put off the old man with talk?"' *Encounters With Kierkegaard*, collected, edited and annotated by Bruce H. Kirmmse and translated with Virginia R. Laursen (Princeton, 1996), p. 100.
9. Transcripts of that request and of related communications can be found in Henrik Rosenmeier's translation of Kierkegaard's *Letters and Documents* (LD 23).
10. It is interesting that just as Notabene's wife is portrayed as finding these ideas of her husband quite mad, so on the religious side of the pseudonymous authorship we have from Anti-Climacus a worry – he presents it as a worry in Christianity – that the wife of one who wants to be a Christian in a strong sense will want him to *stop all this lunacy*. But, knowing that St Paul has allowed for marriage, Anti-Climacus confines himself to saying: 'Christianity has an uneasiness about marriage and also desires to have among its many married servants an unmarried person, someone who is single, because Christianity is well aware that with woman and erotic love [*Elskov*] etc. also come all the weaker softer elements in a person, and that insofar as the husband himself does not hit upon them, the wife ordinarily represents them with an unconstraint that is extremely dangerous for

the husband, especially for the one who is to serve Christianity in the stricter sense' (PA 117–118).

11. Steiner's essay can be found in *Kierkegaard: A Critical Reader* edited by Jonathan Rée and Jane Chamberlain (Oxford 1998), p. 105.
12. 'The Second Authorship' is generally taken to encompass *Works of Love* and *Edifying Discourses in Various Spirits* (1847), *The Lily of the Field and the Bird of the Air, Three Discourses at the Communion on Fridays* and *The Sickness unto Death* (1849), *Practice in Christianity* (1850) and *Two Discourses at the Communion on Fridays, For Self-Examination* and *On My Work as an Author* (1851). Unpublished (at the time) work from this phase includes *The Book on Adler* and *The Point of View for My Work as an Author*.
13. See Kirmmse's '"Out with it!": The modern Breakthrough, Kierkegaard and Denmark' in *The Cambridge Companion to Kierkegaard*, edited by Alastair Hannay and Gordon D. Marino (Cambridge, 1998), p. 15.
14. *Peter og Søren Kierkegaard*, I–II, Carl Weltzer (Copenhagen, 1936), I, p. 34.
15. We might also think, though, of what it says in *Practice in Christianity* by way of explanation for Christ's readiness to pay tax in Capernaum (II Matthew 17:24–27). Anti-Climacus, the pseudonymous author of that book, maintains that since 'paying taxes is an unimportant externality, Christ submits to it and guards against offense. It would have been something else with an externality that brazenly claimed to be piety. If Christ had not submitted, he would have provoked their offense, and the reason would quite rightly have been that by withdrawing from the established order a single individual seems to make himself more than human – but from that it still does not follow, to repeat again, that he qualitatively defines himself as being God' (PA 93).
16. *Works of Love* was published in 1847, the year which is generally considered to have been the worst point in the Irish Famine.
17. '"Out with it!": The modern Breakthrough, Kierkegaard and Denmark' in *The Cambridge Companion to Kierkegaard*, edited by Alastair Hannay and Gordon D. Marino (Cambridge, 1998), p. 17.
18. See Paul Ricouer's 'Philosophy after Kierkegaard' in *Kierkegaard: A Critical Reader*, edited by Jonathan Rée and Jane Chamberlain (Oxford, 1998), p. 10.
19. See Croxall's introduction to his own translation of *Johannes Climacus*, or, *De Omnibus Dubitandum Est* and *A Sermon* (Stanford, 1967), p. 28.
20. The conversion is said to have been experienced following a period of deep depression that culminated in Hamann reading the Bible from cover to cover.
21. See 'An Assessment', T. H. Croxall's introduction to his translation of Kierkegaard's *Johannes Climacus* or, *De Omnibus Dubitandum Est* and *A Sermon* (Stanford, 1967), p. 25.
22. Hegel's view is rationalistic to a high degree, his interpretation of the dogma of the Holy Trinity being a case in point: God the Father, and Christ the Son correspond to the universal and particular aspects of

the Concept respectively, with the Holy Spirit corresponding to their unity in the individual aspect. Jamie Turnbull notes: 'For Hegel the incarnation is a point within the system, a point that can be both incorporated and surpassed by the movements of spirit. The consequence of this move, Kierkegaard thinks, is that for Hegel one can be Christian simply in virtue of being acculturated into society.' See Turnbull's essay 'Kierkegaard's Supernaturalism' in *Kierkegaard and Christianity* (*Acta Kierkegaardiana Vol. 3*), edited by Roman Králik, Abrahim Khan, Peter Šajda, Jamie Turnbull and Andrew J. Burgess (Toronto, 2008), p. 76.

23. Some of Kierkegaard's remarks about Schelling can be found in a letter to his friend Emil Boesen as quoted on p. xxiv in the Hongs' 'Historical Introduction' to *The Concept of Irony*.
24. See for example the introduction by Stephen D. Crites to *Søren Kierkegaard: Crisis in the Life of an Actress and Other Essays on Drama* (New York, 1967), p. 18.
25. See for example *Papers and Journals: A Selection*, Søren Kierkegaard, translated with an introduction by Alastair Hannay (Harmondsworth, 1996).
26. One useful edition of these is Søren Kierkegaard, *The Last Years, Journals 1853–1855*, edited and translated by Ronald Gregor Smith (London, 1965).
27. In the preface to *Philosophical Fragments*, pseudonymous author Johannes Climacus asks: 'But what is my opinion?' and answers: 'Do not ask me about that. Next to the question of whether or not I have an opinion, nothing can be of less interest to someone else than what my opinion is. To have an opinion is to me both too much and too little; it presupposes a security and well-being in existence akin to having a wife and children in this mortal life, something not granted to a person who has to be up and about night and day and yet has no fixed income. In the world of spirit, this is my case, for I have trained myself and am training myself always to be able to dance lightly in the service of thought, as far as possible to the honour of the god and for my own enjoyment, renouncing domestic bliss and civic esteem, the *communio bonorum* [community of goods] and the concordance of joys that go with having an opinion' (PF/JC 7).

CHAPTER 2: CENTRAL THEMES AND KEY MOTIFS

1. *Kierkegaard: Construction of the Aesthetic*, translated by Robert Hullot-Kentor (Minnesota, 1989), p. 37.
2. In another piece on the lily and the bird (also taking its cue from those well-known verses in Matthew), to be found among those writings grouped together under the title *Without Authority*, Kierkegaard warns against temporary relief when he writes: 'Underlying the poet's life there is really the despair of being able to become what is wished, and this despair feeds *the wish*. But the wish is the invention of disconsolateness.

To be sure, the wish consoles for a moment, but on closer inspection it is evident that it does not console, and therefore we say that the wish is the consolation that disconsolateness invents' (WA 8).

3. As is noted by Søren Landkildehus, Kierkegaard had a special fascination with Friday services as distinct from Sunday services. See 'Through a Veil of Tears: The image of Christ in Kierkegaard's Discourses on *The Woman Who Was a Sinner*' in *Kierkegaard and Christianity* (*Acta Kierkegaardiana Vol. 3*), edited by Roman Králik, Abrahim Kahn, Peter Šajda, Jamie Turnbull and Andrew J. Burgess (Toronto, 2008), p. 133.

CHAPTER 3: IMMEDIACY

1. Later, in *Concluding Unscientific Postscript*, Climacus makes the following observation about Lessing: 'It is the transition, the direct transition from historical reliability to an eternal decision, that Lessing continually contests. Therefore he takes the position of making a distinction between reports of miracles and prophecies—and contemporaneity with these' (CUP 96). He says that Lessing has left himself no opportunity 'to raise the dialectical issue of whether contemporaneity would be of some help, whether it could be more than an *occasion*, which the historical report can also be' (CUP 97). And, restating the case that had been put in *Fragments*, he points out that Lessing's distinction would actually be unfair to the followers who came later (although we can also imagine Kierkegaard thinking that later followers, were the distinction to be upheld, would have a means of evading, or half-evading, the 'infinite requirement' that is placed upon them): '*Fragments*, however, attempted to show that contemporaneity does not help at all, because there is in all eternity no direct transition, which would also have been an unbounded injustice towards all those who came later [. . .]' (CUP 97).
2. Essential reading for those wanting to think earnestly and yet jestingly about the humorist in Kierkegaard and in his authorship is John Lippitt's *Humour and Irony in Kierkegaard's Thought* (Basingstoke, 2000).
3. One of the reservations about the authorship expressed by Kierkegaard's brother, Peter Christian, in his talk at the Roskilde Ecclesiastical Convention of 7 July 1855, concerns the degree of patience and sympathy extended by the pseudonyms towards those whose progress in the faith is patchy and faltering. '[H]ow can what is consciously or unconsciously present in a large part of that [pseudonymous] literature be defended in its desire to frighten and punish all those who, perhaps in all honesty, are on their way from Haran in Mesopotamia and are drawing nigh to the land of Canaan? Who perhaps stumble [?] every day but who also make daily progress in their pilgrimage? Doesn't the manner in which the Saviour accepts the beginnings of faith, whose frailty he can see a great deal more clearly than can any pseudonym, form a striking contrast?' *Encounters with Kierkegaard*, edited by Bruce

H. Kirmmse and translated by Kirmmse and Virginia R. Laursen (Princeton, 1996), p. 261. Certainly there is no shortage of stern warnings across the authorship about *bad beginnings*. Of course, as it is true that *you have to start somewhere*, there is a danger of taking refuge in the *understandable imperfections* of the start which, combined with an awareness that to be constantly starting (as opposed to taking anything for granted) is on some level a virtue, could lead to a comfortably poor performance. Moreover, it could be argued in Søren's defence that falling short, however inevitable, could not actually be included in the pseudonyms' presentation of *the requirement*.

CHAPTER 4: ETHICS AND LOVE

1. See M. Jamie Ferreira, *Love's Grateful Striving* (Oxford, 2001), p. 5.
2. 'He started full sail on his authorship, producing first Vol. II of *Either/Or*. This is a moving fact, because Vol. II is a telling *apologia* for Marriage, which state S.K. himself was declining.' See T. H. Croxall's introduction to his translation of *Johannes Climacus* or, *De Omnibus Dubitandum Est* and *A Sermon* (Stanford, 1967), p. 45.
3. 'In *Either/Or* [Kierkegaard] has Judge William arguing for an ethic of social conformity, but more typical of Kierkegaard – what we think of as most deeply Kierkegaardian – is the passionate call for individual responsibility.' Anthony Rudd, *Kierkegaard and the Limits of the Ethical* (Oxford, 1993), p. 117.
4. See for example, Ferreira's chapter 'Love's Asymmetry' in *Love's Grateful Striving* (Oxford 2001), pp. 209–227, and my own chapter 'Working through Love: The Subjunctive Hopes All Things' in *Kierkegaard and Levinas: The Subjunctive Mood* (Farnham, 2010), pp. 153–174.
5. Josiah Thompson, *Kierkegaard* (London, 1974), pp. 164–165.
6. Josiah Thompson, *Kierkegaard* (London, 1974), p. 165.
7. T. W. Adorno, *Kierkegaard: Construction of the Aesthetic*, translated and edited by Robert Hullot-Kentor (Minnesota, 1989), p. 40.
8. The much emphasized universality of this 'ethical' that might be about to undergo a 'teleological suspension' would be seen as connected specifically to the universalizing element of the categorical imperative as described in Kant's *Critique of Practical Reason*.
9. Those finding the Hegelian element to be the most obvious key to what *Fear and Trembling* means by 'the ethical' would mention Hegel's notion of *Sittlichkeit* – morality as produced through culture, and shaped by practice and precedent. Judge Wilhelm's letters in the second volume of *Either/Or* are often taken to be putting the case for *Sittlichkeit*.
10. See, for example, in the Routledge Philosophy Guidebook series, John Lippitt's *Kierkegaard and Fear and Trembling* (London, 2003), a work that, in addition to providing the ideal introduction for newcomers, contains countless fresh insights for the already-initiated. See also Clare Carlisle's chapter '*Fear and Trembling*: Faith Beyond Reason' in *Kierkegaard: A Guide for the Perplexed* (London, 2006), pp. 110–131.

11. 'Johannes's description of Abraham poses a sharp challenge to those who would make sense of *Fear and Trembling* as a study in ethics. On the one hand, Johannes does not shrink from depicting Abraham as fully outside the ethical—as truly the murderer of his son. Not only does his conduct violate one of our most important ethical norms, it cannot be justified in any way.' See Green's essay '"Developing" *Fear and Trembling*' in *The Cambridge Companion to Kierkegaard*, edited by Alastair Hannay and Gordon D. Marino (Cambridge, 1998), p. 263.
12. We might, according to Clare Carlisle, 'regard sin in terms of a wrong relationship to ourselves, as falling short of what we know to be our potential, or as neglecting an ideal that we hold to be central to our lives.' *Kierkegaard: A Guide for the Perplexed* (London, 2006), p. 92.
13. M. Jamie Ferreira, *Love's Grateful Striving* (Oxford, 2001), p. 5.
14. Theodor W. Adorno, *Kierkegaard: Construction of the Aesthetic*, translated and edited by Robert Hullot-Kentor (Minnesota, 1989), p. 31.
15. We know that there appear to be some good reasons for *not* wanting God as a middle term, where God is to taken to be all-powerful. Some of these reasons might be quite Kierkegaardian in character. Or, at any rate, there are reasons for supposing that if God exists he cannot be loving. Imagine, for example, that we have learned of a family who are the victims of a terrible disaster. Now while we might decide that what *we ourselves as single individuals* have suffered in this world counts for little, can be transcended, leads to a greater good, or can be viewed as part of an ongoing struggle with a God, we cannot really make such decisions on behalf of this family. Dare we assert that there is a loving and omnipotent God in the face of the harm this family has undergone? How can any philosopher say that these horrors constitute a scar of history that will eventually heal over, or (more offensive still) that it is a necessary moment in the passage towards an as yet unknown good? By the same token, however, we should not object if it is at all a comfort to the friends of this family to suppose that its members are mysteriously being protected from the suffering that we as onlookers must fear would accompany this worst of situations. In fact, let us hope that they *have* been mysteriously anaesthetized, whether it be by God, the Holy Spirit, or by any other means, including, for want of anything better, sheer unconsciousness. All in all, we may not understand what the indicative statement 'God exists' or, for that matter, the statement 'God does not exist' might mean. But perhaps we can understand what the subjunctive statement 'May God protect this person' means. Credit and thanks are due to Philip Mularo, who suggested (in conversation) this tentative approach to faith – faith persisting (or even emerging for the first time) as hope – when confronting disaster and, more generally, in the face of the misery-stricken world as such.
16. This humanism fits into a French tradition of searching for an ethics in a world without God that emerges in the Enlightenment and that may be associated with Voltaire and Rousseau especially.
17. Characters like Jean Tarrou and Dr Bernard Rieux fight against the plague alongside the priest, Père Paneloux, in the classic novel by Albert Camus.

18. Paper delivered at the Annual General Meeting of the UK Søren Kierkegaard Society, held at Christ Church Oxford, 3 May 2008. Pattison attributes the idea to Lev Shestov.
19. Kierkegaard's Jutland Priest, anyway, counsels against such approaches: 'There is nothing edifying in recognizing that God is always in the right, and neither, therefore, in any thought that necessarily follows from it. In that case, when you recognize that God is always in the right, you are standing outside God, and similarly when in consequence you recognize that you are always in the wrong. If on the other hand, on the strength of no precedent recognition you claim, and are convinced, that you are always in the wrong, you are hidden in God. This is your divine worship, your religious devotion, your reverence for God' (Han. EO 605; EOII 350).
20. See Chapter 4 ('Reason and Faith in Kierkegaard') of Brand Blanshard's *Reason and Belief* (London, 1974), pp. 187–247.
21. See Brand Blanshard's *Reason and Belief* (London, 1974), p. 197. 'If sin is everywhere, then it is nowhere in particular. By making everything sinful, the dogma in effect makes sin trivial.'

CHAPTER 5: DESPAIR AND HOPE

1. Readers may wish to consult the relevant chapters in John D. Caputo's *How to Read Kierkgaard* (London, 2007), pp. 9–20, and also Clare Carlisle's *Kierkegaard: A Guide for the Perplexed* (London, 2006), pp. 63–89.
2. George Eliot, *Silas Marner* (London, 1980), p. 25.
3. 'But sometimes it happened that Marner, pausing to adjust an irregularity in his thread, became aware of the small scoundrels, and, though chary of his time, he liked their intrusions so ill that he would descend from his loom, and opening the door, would fix on them a gaze that was always enough to make them take to their legs in terror. For how was it possible to believe that those large brown protuberant eyes in Silas Marner's pale face really saw nothing very distinctly that was not close to them, and not rather that their dreadful stare could dart cramp, or rickets, or a wry mouth at any boy who happened to be in the rear?' George Eliot, *Silas Marner* (London, 1980), p. 16.
4. In discussion during the one-day conference 'Kierkegaard and Modern European Thought' hosted by Michael Weston and the UK Søren Kierkegaard Society held at Essex University on Saturday, 11 May 2002.

CHAPTER 6: HIS CONTINUING RELEVANCE: COMMUNITY AND THE INDIVIDUAL

1. There is clearly a sense in which Kierkegaard's particular antipathy towards 'the crowd' *was* fairly timeless, as is indicated by the following passage – interesting in more ways than one – from an article by Leo

Stan: 'It is interesting to realize that individuality as a modern social-political construct is considered by Kierkegaard, from a *theological perspective*, proto-sinful. For him the excessive cultivation of immanent personhood goes against the truth that the human self received its existence from an immeasurably higher authority. Moreover the way Kierkegaard interprets (and inveighs) the etiology of crowds is neither modern-liberal nor conservative, but rather *soteriological*: humans congregate in masses because, by virtue of their sinful nature, they first and foremost flee the religious obligations of their personal existence.' See: 'God's Exacting Agape of Singular Individuals: A Kierkegaardian Corrective' in *Kierkegaard and Christianity*, edited by Roman Králik, Abrahim Khan, Peter Šajda, Jamie Turnbull and Andrew J. Burgess (Toronto, 2008), pp. 142–143.

2. Indeed, there are what might seem like 'unguarded' moments when Kierkegaard seems to become just a touch haughty, moments when he drifts away from what in *Two Ages* could almost count as 'technical' uses of terms like 'nobody' and 'nobodies' – for the eerily ungraspable agents of an anonymous but unstoppable and unrepentant 'public' – and into a more bog-standard put-down way of using such words: 'A good-natured nobody suddenly becomes a hero "on principle," and the situation is just as comical as a man would be – or everyone if it became the style – if he were to go round wearing a cap with a thirty-foot visor' (TA 101).
3. Alastair Hannay, *Kierkegaard* (London, 1991), p. 281.
4. For example: 'So the son learns that death awaits him – as a punishment, for his existence is crime and transgression. He learns that this life is to be [. . .] a prison, that the world lies in the grip of evil, that God wishes him to hate himself, and that if he does not wish what God wishes, eternal punishment awaits him' (LY 268).
5. All theories of the good that lack at least some awareness of the question of whether, in the first place, it is good to exist at all, could perhaps be regarded as incomplete. At any rate, most theories of how we should live do operate as relative to an assumption that it is good to live. This is not to say there could never be a theory of how best to live after having accepted that reproduction is wrong or even having reproduced, thereby falling short of what Kierkegaard refers to as 'the ideal'. With the latter case we would be in a realm of contingency arrangements and damage limitation somewhat analogous to the one St Paul is in when he is explaining what to do if you really must marry.
6. It is also possible that Kierkegaard was experiencing at that point in his life a severe loneliness – the suffering of which he speaks so often in those last years may not have been altogether 'religious' – and there may have been a growing awareness that a practical problem for his own existence was looming: he was running out of money. This is not to imply that the ideas he was propounding about reproduction as evil are not intellectually serious, however radical they may appear. He had also, by this time, discovered Schopenhauer. But as time went on Kierkegaard

(who periodically scaled down his living arrangements) was increasingly compelled to depend upon his own God-relation, upon grace and upon his faith in the providential – 'governance' – for that spaciousness of which he may formerly at least have enjoyed a semblance (since it would have been *merely* concrete), in *this* world. As regards money, Adorno writes: '[Kierkegaard] stands in opposition to the progress of economic competition that made his type almost extinct. Only an agrarian, economically underdeveloped country could initially guarantee him security and make possible his particular style of life. According to Geismar, Kierkegaard spurned – on the basis of religious scruple – any interest bearing investment of his small estate and instead consumed it in instalments.' Theodor W. Adorno, *Kierkegaard: Construction of the Aesthetic*, translated and edited by Robert Hullot-Kentor (Minnesota, 1989), p. 48.

7. See especially *Kierkegaard: The Self in Society*, edited by George Pattison and Steven Shakespeare (London, 1998).
8. Alastair Hannay, *Kierkegaard* (London, 1991), p. 283.
9. Josiah Thompson, *Kierkegaard* (London, 1974), p. 119.
10. 'When we see a large family packed into a small apartment and yet we see it inhabiting a cozy, friendly spacious apartment – we say it is an upbuilding sight because we see the love that must be in each and every individual, since of course one unloving person would already be enough to occupy the whole place. We say it because we see that there actually is room where there is heart-room. On the other hand, it is scarcely upbuilding to see a restless soul inhabit a place without finding rest in a single one of the many spacious rooms, and yet without being able to spare or do without the smallest cubbyhole.' This is from 'Love Builds Up', at the start of the second series of Christian deliberations in the form of discourses (WoL 224).
11. The Great Irish Famine, as it is sometimes called, caused the population of Ireland to be reduced by a quarter between 1845 and 1852. Approximately one million people are thought to have emigrated and an estimated one million people died of starvation.
12. The idea of turning things around in this way appears in my own *Kierkegaard and Levinas: The Subjunctive Mood* (Farnham, 2010), p. 215.
13. See for example, the third chapter 'Moral Perfectionism and Exemplars' of Lippitt's *Humour and Irony in Kierkegaard's Thought* (London, 2000), pp. 27–66. For specific focus upon the imitation of Christ, see also the second subsection (entitled 'Andrew Cross: Admiration and Imitation') of the seventh chapter of *Kierkegaard and Fear and Trembling*, John Lippitt (London, 2003), pp. 180–194, in the Routledge Philosophy Guidebook series.
14. M. Jamie Ferreira, *Love's Grateful Striving* (Oxford, 2001), p. 25.
15. See, for example, Theodor Haecker: 'But just as Kierkegaard's passionate nature often led him to treat the things of this life too cavalierly, for they embittered him by weighing too heavily upon him when they entered into the causality of his life, so in this case, if they did not blind him to the other great principle [the category of 'the individual' being the first

mentioned] of Christianity, that of community, they only let him see it in a spiritual sense, as the communion of saints, and hindered its realization in the visible Church and its sacraments.' *Søren Kierkegaard*, translated by Alexander Dru (Oxford, 1937), p. 63.

16. Alastair Hannay, *Kierkegaard* (London, 1991), p. 284.
17. Alastair Hannay, *Kierkegaard* (London, 1991), p. 279.
18. T. W. Adorno, *Kierkegaard: Construction of the Aesthetic*, translated and edited by Robert Hullot-Kentor (Minnesota, 1989), pp. 49–50.
19. 'To Preserve One's Soul in Patience' (EUD 181–203) and 'Patience in Expectancy' (EUD 205–226).
20. T. W. Adorno, *Kierkegaard: Construction of the Aesthetic*, translated and edited by Robert Hullot-Kentor (Minnesota, 1989), pp. 50–51.
21. T. W. Adorno, *Kierkegaard: Construction of the Aesthetic*, translated and edited by Robert Hullot-Kentor (Minnesota, 1989), p. 38.
22. Josiah Thompson, *Kierkegaard* (London, 1974), p. 222.
23. Of course, this rests to a degree upon Adorno's ability to perform a kind of psychoanalysis upon the philosophy itself, unearthing that which might be latent, residual or otherwise unconscious in the concepts themselves. At least, that is what comes to mind when Adorno attributes *recognitions*: 'Kierkegaard recognized the distress of incipient high-capitalism. He opposed its privations in the name of a lost immediacy that he sheltered in subjectivity. He analyzed neither the necessity and legitimacy of reification nor the possibility of its correction. But he did nevertheless – even if he was more foreign to the social order than any other idealistic thinker – note the relation of reification and the commodity form in a metaphor that need only be taken literally to correspond with Marxist theories.' T. W. Adorno, *Kierkegaard: Construction of the Aesthetic*, translated and edited by Robert Hullot-Kentor (Minnesota, 1989), p. 39. Other commentators have made the connection with Marx from a different angle – by starting with the immediate affinities and then qualifying them as necessary: 'Kierkegaard would agree with the Marxian of leftist thinkers, that fighting poverty and alleviating the sufferings of the destitute are not frivolous matters. At the same time, as a consistent *Christian* thinker, he would immediately add that such praiseworthy endeavours must be inwardly and individually rooted in an appropriate stance towards God and Christ.' See 'God's Exacting Agape of Singular Individuals: A Kierkegaardian Corrective' by Leo Stan in *Kierkegaard and Christianity* (*Acta Kierkegaardiana Vol. 3*), edited by Králik, Khan, Šajda, Turbull and Burgess (Toronto, 2008), p. 147.
24. See 'Cities of the Dead: the relation of Person and Polis in Kierkegaard's *Works of Love*' in *Kierkegaard: The Self in Society*, edited by George Pattison and Steven Shakespeare (London, 1998), pp. 125–138.
25. T. W. Adorno, *Kierkegaard: Construction of the Aesthetic*, translated and edited by Robert Hullot-Kentor (Minnesota, 1989), p. 39.
26. Josiah Thompson, *Kierkegaard* (London, 1974), p. 83.
27. Josiah Thompson, *Kierkegaard* (London, 1974), p. 219.
28. 'The change in him was obvious to his friends and acquaintances. Regine saw him for the last time in April, and the impression he made

upon her was so strong that she remembered it for half a century. She was leaving for the West Indies with her husband, and on the morning of her departure she passed Kierkegaard in the street. There was something about his look that made her say to him, "God bless you. I hope things go well for you." And he, for the first time since their engagement, raised his wide-brimmed hat and gave her a warm greeting. Hans Brøchner saw him later that summer and noticed a similar transformation.' Josiah Thompson, *Kierkegaard* (London, 1974), p. 228.

29. Josiah Thompson, *Kierkegaard* (London, 1974), p. xvi.
30. Of course Kierkegaard had no great interest in the value of *health* as Josiah Thompson illustrates in *Kierkegaard* (London, 1974), p. 213.
31. He made it his business in that he made it his task, but it is also worth mentioning Josiah Thompson's report that, contrary to what is widely assumed, Kierkegaard did make reasonably tidy sums on the sales of his books – not that this should any way be held against him, for all the tenor of those books may have been anti-materialistic. At any rate, Kierkegaard, would be protected in his own eyes – and quite probably in ours – from any charge of conflicting interests, by an observation that he was a poet, not a priest. But most people, then and now, would probably not even object to a priest making money from a publication.
32. We say 'dialectically' here precisely in order to be Kierkegaardian in our understanding of what it means religiously to give thanks: that the grateful person is not meant, by giving thanks for any worldly sparing of misfortune, to be implying that he or she would be uttering curses if he or she had not been spared, the opposition in this dialectical relation is not between the good fortune and *its* opposite, but rather between giving thanks for something on one hand *and yet* praying for the strength to be able also to give thanks *for something*, in the *opposite situation* of sustaining the loss, or of not being spared persecution or of not having avoided whatever misfortune is at this moment the object of gratitude.
33. There is no bitterness in evidence towards the ordained in *Discourses for Imagined Occasions*, for example, and it is a relevant example because this is a text that deals explicitly with administered rites like matrimony and confession (recognized as sacraments in the Catholic and Anglican faiths although not by the Lutheran Church). Moreover, Kierkegaard considered becoming a pastor himself in 1846.
34. 'The fact that Kierkegaard had gained a measure of happiness through his attack did not mean that it was succeeding. By late September with the ninth issue of *The Instant*, it was obvious to everyone that Kierkegaard's campaign was becoming increasingly repetitive. It had created something of a stir in intellectual circles – Troels-Lund recalled that several students gathered regularly in his brother's room to read and discuss the latest issue of *The Instant*. But the general public had been left offended and uncomprehending.' Josiah Thompson, *Kierkegaard* (London, 1974), pp. 228–229.

35. Could the question 'How much, then, is the little that a person needs?' ever be a question for *research*? Well, perhaps it actually could and should always be a question for research. It may have been a piece of unkindness – an absent-mindedness in respect of the neighbour, no less – that Kierkegaard never wanted to address that, as if everything to do with the indicative was beneath – not him personally – but beneath the single individual who must *alone* be ethical, who must *alone* fall in love, become religious or confront his or her mortality. But it is not as if a person's individuality would be compromised were he or she to regard a survey – conducted very much *in the third person* – into what a person needs as being just as worthwhile. It might be just as worthwhile as a campaign to get everybody to put the question to themselves – which is not to say that it was unkindness on Kierkegaard's part for his discourse to have got me to put it to myself, or you to put it to yourself, dear reader.

BIBLIOGRAPHY

PRIMARY SOURCES: KIERKEGAARD IN TRANSLATION

Kierkegaard, Søren A. *Kierkegaard's Writings*, 26 volumes, ed. Howard Hong and trans. Howard V. Hong and Edna H. Hong, Julia Watkin (for *Early Polemical Writings*), Reidar Tompt and Albert B. Anderson (for *The Concept of Anxiety*) and Todd W. Nichol (for *Prefaces*) (Princeton: Princeton University Press, 1978–).

— *Søren Kierkegaard's Journals and Papers*, 7 volumes, ed. and trans. Howard V. Hong and Edna H. Hong (Bloomington: Indiana University Press, 1967–1978). Assisted by Gregor Malantschuk. Index, Volume 7, by Nathaniel Hong and Charles Baker (Bloomington and London: Indiana University Press, volume 1: 1967; volume 2: 1970; volumes 3 and 4: 1975; volumes 5–7: 1978).

Details of individual works by Kierkegaard, including alternative translations (to the Hongs' edition) by Alastair Hannay, Walter Lowrie, Lee Capel, Stephen Crites, Ronald C. Smith, William McDonald, Douglas V. Steere, David F. Swenson, Lillian Marvin Swenson Alexander Dru, A. S. Aldworth and W. S. Ferrie and others are as follows:

— *Armed Neutrality* and *An Open Letter*, trans. Howard V. Hong and Edna H. Hong (Bloomington and London: Indiana University Press, 1968).

— *Kierkegaard's Attack upon Christendom* (1854–1855), trans. Walter Lowrie (Princeton: Princeton University Press, 1944).

— *On Authority and Revelation, The Book on Adler*, trans. Walter Lowrie (Princeton: Princeton University Press, 1955).

— *Crisis in the Life of an Actress*, trans. Stephen Crites (New York: Harper and Row, 1967).

— *Christian Discourses*, including *The Crisis (and a Crisis) in the Life of an Actress*, trans. Howard V. Hong and Edna H. Hong (Princeton: Princeton University Press, 1997).

— *Christian Discourses*, including 'The Lilies of the Field and the Birds of the Air' and 'Three Discourses at the communion on Fridays', trans. Walter Lowrie (London and New York: Oxford University Press, 1939).

— *The Concept of Anxiety*, trans. Reidar Thomte and Albert B. Anderson (Princeton: Princeton University Press, 1980).

— *The Corsair Affair*, trans. Howard V. Hong and Edna H. Hong (Princeton: Princeton University Press, 1982).
— *Concluding Unscientific Postscript to* Philosophical Fragments, 2 volumes, trans. Howard V. Hong and Edna H. Hong (Princeton: Princeton University Press, 1992).
— *Either/Or*, 2 volumes, trans. Howard V. Hong and Edna. H. Hong (Princeton: Princeton University Press, 1987).
— *Early Polemical Writings*, trans. Julia Watkin (Princeton: Princeton University Press, 1990).
— *Eighteen Upbuilding Discourses*, trans. Howard V. Hong and Edna H. Hong (Princeton: Princeton University Press, 1990).
— *Fear and Trembling* and *Repetition*, trans. Howard V. Hong and Edna H. Hong (Princeton: Princeton University Press, 1983).
— *For Self-Examination* and *Judge for Yourself!*, trans. Howard V. Hong and Edna H. Hong (Princeton: Princeton University Press, 1990).
— *Johannes Climacus or De Omnibus Dubitandum Est* and *A Sermon*, trans. T. H. Croxall (Stanford: Stanford University Press, 1958).
— *The Journals of Søren Kierkegaard*, trans. Alexander Dru (London and New York: Oxford University Press, 1938).
— *A Kierkegaard Reader: Texts and Narratives*, eds. Roger Poole and Henrik Stangerup (London: Fourth Estate, 1989).
— *The Last Years*, translated by Ronald C. Smith (New York: Harper Row, 1965).
— *Letters and Documents*, trans. Howard V. Hong and Edna H. Hong (Princeton: Princeton University Press, 2009).
— *Papers and Journals: A Selection*, ed. and trans. Alastair Hannay (Harmondsworth: Penguin, 1996).
— *Parables of Kierkegaard*, ed. Thomas C. Oden and illustrated by Lonni Sue Johnson (Princeton: Princeton University Press, 1989).
— *Philosophical Fragments* and *Johannes Climacus*, trans. Howard V. Hong and Edna H. Hong (Princeton: Princeton University Press, 1985).
— *The Point of View for My Work as an Author*, trans. Walter Lowrie (London and New York: Oxford University Press, 1939).
— *Practice in Christianity*, trans. Howard V. Hong and Edna H. Hong. (Princeton: Princeton University Press, 1991).
— *Prefaces/Writing Sampler*, ed. and trans. Todd W. Nichol (Princeton: Princeton University Press, 1997).
— *Prefaces: Light Reading for Certain Classes as the Occasion May Require*, trans. William McDonald (Tallahassee: Florida State University Press, 1989).
— *The Present Age*, trans. Alexander Dru and introduced by Walter Kaufmann (New York: Harper Torchbooks, 1962).
— *Purity of Heart of Heart is to Will One Thing*, trans. Douglas V. Steere (New York: Harper Torchbooks, 1956).
— *Repetition*, trans. Walter Lowrie (Princeton: Princeton University Press, 1964).
— *The Sickness unto Death*, trans. Howard V. Hong and Edna H. Hong. (Princeton: Princeton University Press, 1980).

— *Stages on Life's Way*, trans. Howard V. Hong and Edna H. Hong (Princeton: Princeton University Press, 1989).

— *Thoughts on Crucial Situations in Human Life: Three Discourses on Imagined Occasions* trans. D. F. Swenson and ed. L. M. Swenson (Minneapolis: Augsburg, 1941).

— *Three Discourses on Imagined Occasions*, trans. Howard V. Hong and Edna H. Hong (Princeton: Princeton University Press, 1993).

— *Traité du désespoir*, trans. Knud Ferlov and Jean-J. Gateau (Paris: Gallimard, 1949).

— *Two Ages: The Age of Revolution and The Present Age. A Literary Review*, trans. Howard V. Hong and Edna H. Hong (Princeton: Princeton University Press, 1978).

— *Upbuilding Discourse in Various Spirits*, translated by Howard V. Hong Hong and Edna H. Hong (Princeton: Princeton University Press, 1993).

— *Works of Love*, trans. Howard V. Hong and Edna H. Hong (Princeton: Princeton University Press, 1995).

— *Works of Love*, trans. D. F. Swenson and L. M. Swenson (London: Oxford University Press, 1946).

SECONDARY LITERATURE ON KIERKEGAARD

Adorno, Theodor W., *Kierkegaard: Construction of the Aesthetic*, ed. and trans. Robert Hullot-Kentor (Minneapolis: University of Minnesota Press, 1989). See also *Kierkegaard: Konstruktion des Ästhetischen* (Frankfurt am Main: Suhrkamp Verlag, 1962), first published in 1933.

Blanshard, Brand, 'Reason and Faith in Kierkegaard' in *Reason and Belief* (Oxford: Allen & Unwin, 1974), pp. 187–247.

Colette, Jacques, *Kierkegaard at la Non-Philosophie* (Paris: Gallimard, 1994).

Creegan, Charles L., *Wittgenstein and Kierkegaard: Religion, Individuality and Philosophical Method* (London: Routledge, 1989).

Diem, Hermann, *Kierkegaard's Dialectic of Existence*, trans. Harold Knight (Edinburgh: Oliver & Boyd, 1959). See also *Die Existenzdialectik von Søren Kierkegaard* (Zollikon-Zürich: Evangelischer Verlag A. G., 1950).

Ferreira, M. Jamie, *Transforming Vision: Imagination and Will in Kierkegaardian Faith* (Oxford: Clarendon Press, 1991).

— 'Faith and the Kierkegaardian leap' in *The Cambridge Companion to Kierkegaard*, eds. Alastair Hannay and Gordon Marino (Cambridge: Cambridge University Press, 1998), pp. 207–234.

Friedmann, Rudolph, 'Kierkegaard: The Analysis of the Psychological Personality' in *Horizon*, ed. Cyril Connolly (Volume VIII, No. 46, October, 1943), pp. 252–273.

Grimsley, Ronald, *Søren Kierkegaard and French Literature* (Cardiff: University of Wales Press, 1966).

Hannay, Alastair, *Kierkegaard* (London: Routledge, 1993).

Hartshorne, Marion Homes, *Kierkegaard, Godly Deceiver* (New York: Columbia University Press, 1990).

Jackson, Timothy, 'Arminian edification: Kierkegaard on grace and free will' in *The Cambridge Companion to Kierkegaard*, ed. Alastair Hannay and Gordon Marino (Cambridge: Cambridge University Press, 1998), pp. 235–256.

Law, David R., *Kierkegaard as Negative Theologian* (Oxford: Clarendon Press, 1993).

Lippitt, John, *Humour and Irony in Kierkegaard's Thought* (London: Macmillan, 2000).

— *Kierkegaard and* Fear and Trembling (London: Routledge, 2003).

Kirmmse, Bruce H. (ed. and trans. with Virginia R. Laursen), *Encounters With Kierkegaard: A Life as Seen by His Contemporaries* (Princeton: Princeton University Press, 1996).

Mackey, Louis, 'The Poetry of Inwardness' in *Kierkegaard: A Collection of Critical Essays*, ed. Josiah Thompson (New York, 1972).

Maheu, René (editor), *Kierkegaard vivant* (Paris: Gallimard, 1966).

Malantschuk, Gregor, *Kierkegaard's Thought*, ed. and trans. Howard V. Hong and Edna H. Hong (Princeton: Princeton University Press, 1974).

Marino, Gordon (ed. with Alastair Hannay), *The Cambridge Companion to Kierkegaard* (Cambridge: Cambridge University Press, 1998).

Matuštík, Martin Joseph and Westphal, Merold (eds.), *Kierkegaard in Post/Modernity* (Bloomington: Indiana University Press, 1995).

McCarthy, Vincent A., *The Phenomenology of Moods in Kierkegaard* (The Hague: Kluwer Academic Publishers, 1978).

Mullen, John Douglas, *Kierkegaard's Philosophy: Self-Deception and Cowardice in the Present Age* (New York: University Press of America, 1981).

Nagy, András, 'Abraham the Communist' in *Kierkegaard: The Self in Society*, eds. George Pattison and Steven Shakespeare (London: Macmillan, 1998), pp. 196–220.

Pattison, George, *Kierkegaard: The Aesthetic and the Religious: From the Magic theatre to the Crucifixion of the Image* (New York: St. Martin's Press, 1992).

— *Agnosis: Theology and the Void* (London: Macmillan, 1996).

— *Kierkegaard and the Crisis of Faith* (London: SPCK, 1997).

— *Art, Faith and Modernity* (London: Macmillan, 1998).

— *'Poor Paris!' – Kierkegaard's Critique of the Spectacular City* (Berlin: Walter de Gruyter, 1999).

— *Kierkegaard on Art and Communication* (ed.) (New York, 1992).

— 'Kierkegaard: Aesthetics and "The Aesthetic" in *The British Journal of Aesthetics*, Volume 31, Number 2 (Oxford, April 1991).

— 'On Reading Kierkegaard Religiously: A Reply to Michael Strawser' *The Søren Kierkegaard Newsletter* (published by the International Kierkegaard Centre in Northfield, Minnesota), Number 36, July, 1998, p. 12.

— 'Art in an age of reflection' in *The Cambridge Companion to Kierkegaard*, eds. Alastair Hannay and Gordon Marino (Cambridge: Cambridge University Press, 1998), pp. 76–100.

— 'The Theory and Practice of Language and Communiucation in Kierkegaard's Upbuilding Discourses' *Kierkegaardiana 19*, ed. Joakim Garff, Arne Grøn, Eberhard Harbsmeier and Bruce Kirmmse (Copenhagen: C. A. Reitzel, 1998), pp. 81–94.

Poole, Roger, *Kierkegaard: The Indirect Communication* (Charlottesville: University of Virginia, 1993).

— (ed. with Henrik Stangerup), *The Laughter Is On My Side: An Imaginative Introduction to Kierkegaard* (Princeton: Princeton University Press, 1989).

Pyper, Hugh, 'Cities of the Dead: the relation of Person and Polis in Kierkegaard's *Works of Love*' in *Kierkegaard: The Self in Society*, eds. George Pattison and Steven Shakespeare (London: Macmillan, 1998), pp. 125–138.

Rée, Jonathan, *Kierkegaard: A Critical Reader* (ed. with Jane Chamberlain) (Oxford: Blackwell, 1998).

Rohde, Peter P. *Søren Kierkegaard The Danish Philosopher* (Copenhagen: The Press Department of the Danish Ministry for Foreign Affairs).

Rudd, Anthony, *Kierkegaard and the Limits of the Ethical* (Oxford: Clarendon, 1997).

Sartre, Jean-Paul, 'Kierkegaard: The Singular Universal', in his *Between Existentialism and Marxism*, trans. John Mathews (London: Verso, 1983).

Serrano, Susan, *The Will as Protagonist – The Role of the Will in the Existentialist Writings of Miguel de Unamuno: Affinities and with Kierkegaard and Nietzsche* (Sevilla: Padilla, 1996).

Skjoldager, Emanuel, *Søren Kierkegaard og mindesmærkerne* (Copenhagen: C. A. Reitzels Forlag, 1983).

— *Den egentlige Kierkegaard: Søren Kierkegaards syn på kirken og de kirkelige handlinger* (Copenhagen, C. A. Reitzels Forlag, 1982).

Shakespeare, Steven, *Kierkegaard, Language and the Reality of God* (Aldershot: Ashgate, 2001).

— *Kierkegaard: The Self in Society* (ed. with George Pattison) (London: Macmillan, 1998).

Shestov (Chestov), Leon (Lev), *Kierkegaard and the Existentialist Philosophy*, trans. E. Hewitt (Athens: Ohio University Press, 1969).

Søltoft, Pia, *Svimmelhedens etik – om forholdet mellem den enkelte og den anden hos Buber, Lévinas og især Kierkegaard* (Copenhagen: Gad Publishers, 2000).

Stott, Michelle, *Behind the mask: Kierkegaard's Pseudonymic Treatment of Lessing in the* Concluding Unscientific Postsript (London: Associated University Press, 1993).

Thompson, Josiah, *Kierkegaard* (London: Gollancz, 1974).

Thulstrup, Niels, *Kierkegaard's Relation to Hegel*, trans. George L. Stengren (Princeton: Princeton University Press, 1980). See also *Kierkegaards Forhold til Hegel* (Copenhagen: Gyldenal, 1967).

Vardy, Peter, *Kierkegaard* (London: HarperCollins, 1996).

Wahl, Jean, *Études Kierkegaardiennes* (Paris: Vrin, 1949).

Walker, Jeremy, *To Will One Thing: Reflections on Kierkegaard's* Purity of Heart (Montreal: McGill-Queen's University Press, 1972).

Weston, Michael, *Kierkegaard and Modern Continental Philosophy* (London: Routledge, 1994).
Westphal, Merold, *Becoming a Self: A Reading of Kierkegaard's* Concluding Unscientific Postscript (Indiana: Purdue University Press, 1996).
— 'Kierkegaard and Hegel' *The Cambridge Companion to Kierkegaard*, eds. Alastair Hannay and Gordon Marino (Cambridge: Cambridge University Press, 1998), pp. 101–124.
Wirzba, Norman, 'Teaching as a Propaedeutic to Religion: The contribution of Levinas and Kierkegaard', *International Journal for Philosophy of Religion* 39 (Kluwer Academic Publishers, April 1996), pp. 77–94.
Wyschogrod, Michael, *Kierkegaard and Heidegger: The Ontology of Existence* (London: Routledge & Kegan Paul, 1954).

INDEX